Name:

3 Months to Conversational

First Edition

Second Language Strategies

MMXXIII

Copyright © 2024 Second Language Strategies LLC

All rights reserved. No part of this publication may be reproduced, distributed, or transmitted in any form or by any means, including photocopying, recording, or other electronic or mechanical methods, without the prior written permission of the publisher, except in the case of brief quotations embodied in critical reviews and certain other noncommercial uses permitted by copyright law. For permission requests, write to the publisher, addressed "Attention: Permissions Coordinator," at the website below.

www.secondlanguagestrategies.com

Any references to historical events, real people, or real places are used fictitiously. Names, characters, and places are products of the author's imagination.

Printed by Second Language Strategies in the United States of America.

First printing edition 2024.

Table of Contents

Introduction ··· 8-12
Language Recovery ·· 13-19
Localized Immersion ·· 20-47
Pattern Recognition ·· 48-55
Patterns Examples ·· 56-67
Conclusion ··· 68-91
Extras ··· 92-103

Introduction

Making the choice to learn a new language is something that millions of people around the world choose to do every day. Unfortunately, there are just as many people who give up on their second language acquisition temporarily or permanently. Whether that happens because of a bad experience within a classroom or a lack of guidance throughout the challenges of language learning, the goal of this book will be to delineate a clear path for those who truly want to expand their linguistic competencies. While I will not be diving into too many specific exercises, I will be working through my methodology and the approach I have taken with students for the last several years to great success.

That is not to say that this book will be completely devoid of exercises and actionable advice, but for the most part we will be looking at overarching principles that will allow you to enhance and accelerate your second, third, or fourth language acquisition. Over the past decade I have thought about the things that make or break language learners and in the end I was able to isolate three concepts that every language learner should take advantage of throughout the duration of their language learning process.

These core principles are, Language Recovery, Localized Immersion, and Pattern Recognition. However, before we break those down I would like to discuss precisely why it is worthwhile taking these into account. That is to say, why should you listen to anything I have to say in the first place?

I have always been enthralled by languages. From a young age I remember working with sign language and Spanish, crafting sentences and doing what I could to sound as eloquent as possible in both new languages and my first language, English. Writing has always been an outlet for me and learning to write in new languages always brought me a feeling of uncontrollable excitement. My local high school had a well known foreign exchange student program. Every year I gravitated to the new kids from around the world and they seemed to find comfort in my company as well. They would teach me words in their native languages and I would help them improve their English. The relationships were always symbiotic and once I began to travel I realized this feeling would persist irrespective of where in the world I found myself.

    At age 17 I participated in a program called, Modern Language Study Abroad (MLSA) and I flew to Costa Rica alone to stay with a host family and study Spanish at the University of Costa Rica in San Jose. My Spanish at the time was mediocre at best, only two years of Spanish classes in a public education setting. Fortunately, I had learned sign language the year before because when I landed my host family was not at the airport to pick me up. I was unable to speak Spanish well enough to explain my situation and, having expected a welcome party from either the program or my host family, I began to panic. It was my first time out of the country and I had no idea what anyone was saying or what I was to do. After taking a deep breath, I stepped outside thinking my host family might be waiting for me out there. They were not. There was, however, a man using sign language a bit down the road. Though we used slightly different versions, he was able to understand me and called a taxi for me driven by someone who spoke English. This was the first time that knowing more than one language allowed me to communicate with someone to solve a problem. It is more than possible that this initial interaction set in motion my love for travel, languages, and communication, though I believe I was probably already well down that road.

Once I arrived at my host family's house I was surprised to find out that they did not speak any English. You will often hear that immersion is the best way to learn a language, but people rarely discuss how difficult the process is. The exhaustion, frustration, and miscommunication that dictates the first three months should not be understated. However, if you can push through those challenges you will walk away with a new skill that takes many others years to master; and likely some life long friends with whom you will always be able to practice and maintain your new skills.

Though this was my first experience with complete immersion learning, it was not my last. A year later, having had the time of my life learning Spanish and living in Costa Rica, I moved to Belgium with the Rotary Youth Exchange International program. The only difference this time is that I had absolutely no experience with the French language, nor did I understand that there are 3 national languages in Belgium. Rotary is unique in that within the program you will live with not one but two or three different families. My first host family spoke decent English, but my second host family spoke absolutely no English

In this program I was to attend a second senior year of high school, taking all of the same classes as the people my age, getting grades, participating in sports, and integrating in every way possible. I loved every minute of it and by the end of the school year I was able to challenge my classmates in topics from calculus to physics to philosophy. All of these experiences led me to develop the language learning principles that you will see in the next chapters. My goal is for you to be inspired and understand that you can do anything you set your mind to, especially when it comes to learning a new language. More importantly, though, I want to demonstrate that everyone faces the same problems and there are ways to overcome them. As with most things, when it comes to language acquisition, often the best way out is through.

      Once I returned to the USA, I jumped into university and completed my degree in French Translation with a minor in Spanish. My love for languages only grew when I was taking these courses as my professors were all just as passionate about the languages they taught. The experience in university, particularly in higher level courses, is drastically different from the experience in the primary public education system. That is the reason I began working on this business in the first place. Languages are a beautiful part of the world and being able to communicate with people is a gift and it is a gift you can give to yourself at any time.

      So many people have been driven away from this process by inadequate teachers, horrible metrics, and unrealistic expectations. Over the past few years we have shown that anyone can learn a language at any time in their life, you must only make the choice and remain dedicated to consistency even when things get difficult. I have had the pleasure of watching retirees pick up new languages and watching children grow up bilingual. If you have been waiting for a sign to get started on your second language acquisition journey, this is it. Remember, though, there is no reason for you to start at zero. Especially if you have already spent years and years behind a desk working on a second language in school. That's where Language Recovery can help jump start your adventure.

Language Recovery

One of the most perverse myths about learning a new language is that of, "If you don't use it, you will lose it." because it can completely turn people away from learning languages. The truth is, so long as you come back to it with some level of consistency, you will never lose it. Often it is easier to believe something is lost so as to avoid the amount of effort it will take to awaken it. That is the choice you will make when starting your second language acquisition. Do you want to start from zero as if you had never seen the language before or do you want to take time to tap into your latent knowledge so that you can focus on things that move the needle the most?

     I want to make it clear, you know and remember more than you think you do. The idea that your brain just discards all of the information you don't use on a day to day basis is ludicrous. The most important part of this exercise will be reframing the way you view languages and your way of learning and retaining them. You will only "lose it" if you make the decision to never come back to it. One of the more challenging things about this reframing is thinking about where you are and not where you *think* you should be. It is easy to say, "I studied for x years, therefore I should be at y level", however this is simply not how it works. Everyone has their own path and comparing yourself to where others are at in their journey is counterproductive. The only reason to remember where you started is to be able to see how far you've come. This is important for a couple different reasons, not the least of which is understanding what drove you to stop. Was it a bad teacher? Were you working on a language you had no interest in? Were you just young and dumb?

     Understanding what made you stop can serve you in

that you will know what to avoid this time around. Your goal, and mine for you, is to make language learning a part of your everyday routine. In order to do this, you will need to be honest with yourself and do what you can to play to your strengths and mitigate your weaknesses. Everyone learns differently, that's why the education system has failed to teach most people how to acquire a language. Boilerplate courses and one way systems will never be appropriate for hundreds if not thousands of drastically different learning styles.

Now that the things holding you back have been decided, what are some of the things you actually did enjoy about learning another language?

Whether you enjoyed listening to the other language because it was melodic or speaking with others because you were able to connect with new people in a new language, focusing on what you enjoyed will be important as you start over. The goal is to create a system where you stack Ws by doing things you already enjoy. If you love music, search for music in your target language. If you love history, search for history lectures in your target language. If you love to read, find books ranging in difficulty in your target language. Do you spend time watching TV? Watch some series in your target language with subtitles in your native language. If you are doing what you enjoy it becomes a delight to study rather than a drag. For a long time you did not get to choose your study materials, that is no longer the case.

Vocabulary worksheets and pass/fail tests are nothing compared to simulated immersion. You are the only person you can depend on now, assuming you are undertaking this endeavor on your own without a coach. That means it will be on you to put the support infrastructure into place. The advantage to this is that you can choose what you surround yourself with and how you reward yourself.

Some of the support that is provided to the masses by

and large does not do much in the way of keeping people motivated. Part of the issue is that motivation is the goal when discipline should be. If you are disciplined in your language studies you will crush every motivated person on the way to the top. A good starting question is, "What is the minimum that I can do, that I *would* do, day after day and what would I like as a reward for that?"; and once you set the foundation you can build upon it. It is time to set yourself up for success.Now that we have established everything that went wrong and a couple of things that went right, it is time to plug it all in and win. Only you know what will work best for you. You also now know that your language lies dormant, waiting for you to come back and revive it.

     If your goal is to become fluent and work with the language in a professional capacity, the best time to start is now. In a year, doing the right things, you will be well on your way to C2 certification. However, if your goal is to be conversational, you are much closer than you may think. The most challenging part of becoming conversational or fluent will be speaking, unless you live somewhere that allows for total immersion. With that in mind, it is important to facilitate immersion as much as possible. As you begin shopping around for the best language app you will notice they often go back to the idea of simulating immersion. Of course this is the goal, but a computer or phone will never be an adequate replacement for the real thing.

     The best way to set yourself up for success is by finding a native speaker with whom you can practice. It is also imperative that you understand you *will* make mistakes, and lots of them. This is all part of the process. Write down your mistakes, correct them, and continue learning. An advantage you have now over yourself of the past is that you know what did and did not work for you. Now that you are in control you can put more into the things that move the needle the most at your own pace rather than defaulting to what everyone else is told works best. What matters now is that you don't let what you're good at be a reason to avoid what you struggle with in the language. If you love to read but hate to write, you need to spend more time writing. If you hate speaking, you need to speak more. If you struggle to read, you need to read more. Focus on what needs the most improvement when you are recovering, the rest will come.

Millions of people around the world have spent years sitting through language courses to satisfy education requirements in their respective countries. In most of the United States, a second language is a requirement to graduate high school and an additional requirement to graduate from university. However, those language classes are designed to ensure students are able to pass a standardized test. They are not designed to actually help students become bilingual. Too many people spend time memorizing and regurgitating facts throughout their time in the education system. While this may be effective to assure one graduates, it is far from the ideal way to learn anything, let alone a new language.

All that to say, the time spent behind those desks, ignoring the teachers, and doing the bare minimum to get the grade needed were not a complete waste. The brain is an amazing organ and, even if one does not pay particular attention to something, the brain often carves out a place to store the memory. Whether it was five years ago or fifty years ago, there is latent knowledge available to nearly everyone so long as they do the things necessary to unlock it. The more years spent behind a desk repeating the words on the board, the easier it will be to go back and remember all things that were studied. Irrespective of the amount of years, there is dormant knowledge waiting to be awoken.

Here are the steps to making this happen in your life in the same way I run through them with clients:

1. **Collect your notebook, pens, and a bilingual dictionary**
2. **Set a timer on your phone for between 5 and 10 minutes**
   a. **The timer will likely start at 10 minutes and go down to 5 over time as you repeat this exercise.**
3. **Write down everything you can remember from class.**
   a. **Animals, foods, verbs, colors, numbers, greetings, salutations, adjectives, nouns, adverbs**
4. **Repeat steps 2 and 3 up to four times per week for one month.**

As you work through this exercise, one of the things you will notice is that many of the things you remember are tied to memories you have, not necessarily the class or the lessons. Words and phrases that made you laugh, inside jokes you had with your friends, and words you pronounced incorrectly or that led to embarrassing misunderstandings. All of these things work to ensure you are able to recall things with ease. You can use this to amplify your language acquisition in real time, but more on that in the next chapter.

The goal of Language Recovery is to ensure you never have to start at zero. After spending so much time ostensibly learning a new language, you might as well use the things you have learned as a jumping off point. It will be more work the longer it has been since you were in school, but it is worth the effort to awaken this dormant knowledge. A majority of the resources available all start with the same things. This can give the impression that you are not making progress even if you are going into month 8 of your language learning journey. Language learning apps are particularly egregious in this. There is rarely a reason why you should be reviewing colors and numbers when returning to a language after spending years away from it. Chances are you will not remember every number or color or animal, but you do not need to spend an excessive amount of time on those things.

  In a world where efficiency is paramount, focusing on the things you need to learn in order to begin speaking is crucial. Working on a bit of Language Recovery will make clear the areas of weakness you have. From there you can really zero in on where you need to place your focus. Whether that is learning terms and phrases related to your career, learning how to flirt, or learning specialized language to give yourself an advantage when visiting or moving to a new country. If you are struggling to get through these exercises, take some time to look around you. It never ceases to amaze me just how many foreign languages are all around us nowadays.

  Unless one is fluent in more than one language it is easy to miss just how many languages floating around in the outside world. From menus to marketing, chances are the language you are learning is written somewhere around you in one of the places you frequent.

Just in a Mexican restaurant you will see dozens of words, verde, carne, asada, relleno, camarones, arroz, pollo, ensalada, sopa, gallo, queso, bebidas, and many more. Going to Starbucks you can learn a couple Italian words, opening the spice cabinet you can learn French and German, there are so many loan words in English that there is always something to be gained from going out and looking around.

    If you are struggling to find languages around you, then you are going to need to make it happen yourself. As many know, the best way to learn a new language is through complete immersion. It is the most difficult, but it is also the most effective and efficient. When you are unable to achieve that, the next best step is to create an immersion environment for yourself. There are layers to this exercise, just as with the last, and it is worth working through each one of them. This process is something my clients and I call Localized Immersion.

Localized Immersion

When approaching a new language, the first thing most people think about is what to do first. What the most natural way of learning a language would be for them. These are good questions, but at the end of the day, it has never been disputed and likely never will be that immersion is the best way to learn a language. But what if you don't have the time or the funds to go live in a foreign country for 6-12 months? That's where Localized Immersion comes in and carries the day.

First, what is it?

Localized immersion is language immersion that you create. The way I like to think about it is that by replacing one daily activity you do with an activity you do in your target language (this can be the same activity just *in* the target language), then you will eventually build an environment in which you can only interact with your target language.

What does that look like?

Let's say you are a home chef or even just someone who enjoys cooking, if you're spending time cooking anyway, you should look up some recipes in your target language. This is something I find incredible, you can Google *anything* in your target language that you can google in your mother tongue. All you need to do is type whatever it is you want to read about, watch, study, or listen to into a translation app, unless you can translate it yourself, then copy and paste it into your search engine of choice. You should have plenty of options to choose from and, if you don't, you can take advantage of a virtual private network or VPN to change your computer's registered location. If you are learning Spanish, for example, you can change your location to somewhere in South or Central America to ensure your results are more aligned with your search goals.

As with most study techniques, there are levels to this you can use to progressively overload and ensure consistent progress even through the latter stages of your language acquisition. Assuming you are just starting out, try not to overwhelm yourself. Start with manageable, bit size pieces that you can consistently return to without feeling completely lost. Building up your confidence and gaining momentum in the early stages of learning a new language is absolutely vital. Invariably you will, at one point or another, stagnate and hit a plateau. The momentum you built up leading to that moment will carry you through those times and can be the difference between walking away and reaching fluency. Whether you choose to begin with lullabies, children's stories, comics, or internet memes, spending an hour per day searching for comprehensible input in your target language will become an invaluable skill quickly.

The general issue with learning a foreign language is that there is little to no opportunity to have exposure to it. Limited exposure will delay language learning indefinitely, so the goal is to minimize that. Exposure is the most important thing when building your immersion environment. Again, the toughest part about a foreign language is that it is foreign and therefore not exactly easily accessible. Most immersion programs only work because *there is no option to default out*. You learn the language because you don't have a choice. So, if you want to create an immersion method unique to you, find ways to force yourself into speaking and using the new language. If you can default out, you will. Do not give yourself the option.

Keep in mind, though, foreign language skills develop over time and even with more than partial immersion, it can take months or even a year to learn a new language.

Be gracious with yourself, language acquisition will come with time and continued effort. That said, here are some of the reasons why immersion programs work and immersion in general work so well.Learning to speak a language the way you speak your mother tongue is absolutely vital. It is hard enough to learn a language, there is no reason to learn a new personality as well. That is why immersion is so powerful. When you are living *your* life in the new language, you will learn to use that language in a way specific to you.

     Immersion education focuses, ideally, on learning to do things exclusively in a new language. If you learn something for the first time in a foreign language, you will necessarily have to translate it in your head to understand it, no matter how long it takes. The memory encoding that takes place during this process is important for enhancing language learning. I always say that the best way to learn a language is by doing things that you enjoy. This is especially true when it comes to immersive learning. You are going to be spending hours and hours during your everyday life exposed to the language, you might as well spend the time doing and learning about things in which you are already interested.

     Beyond that, I wanted to discuss a way that many of my German friends immersed themselves in English: Video Games.

Immerse yourself in a digital world!

     While video games in excess are, as with anything, harmful, they also provide a unique opportunity for language learners. Most video games are available in multiple languages, some PC based games allow for you to play through in multiple languages as well. Personally, I played through the entirety of Skyrim in German when I was learning it. I have German friends who all perfected their English playing League of Legends and watching films in English. There is no shame in wanting to spend time doing something you enjoy. However, if you're going to spend hours and hours playing video games, you might as well get some language exposure at the same time! Doing things you enjoy makes being a language learner more fun and when it's fun it's easy. Not only that, but videogames present an opportunity to develop fluency simply through listening and interacting with new grammar and vocabulary. The issue many language learners run into is that vocabulary inputs are often limited. By playing through different video games that take place in different worlds, you will be exposed to all types of vocabulary and grammar combinations.

Remaining Well Rounded

It is important to try and remain as well rounded as possible. Meaning you cannot always be listening, especially not to the same orator. You need to be reading, writing, speaking, translating, **and** listening. One of my favorite exercises for this is listening to and translating songs. Learning a new language by listening to music is fantastic. Unlike most things, generally speaking most people have heard music in a different language. If you want to differentiate yourself from the average language learners you are going to want to add an extra step. Looking up the lyric video and watching through it will ensure you can actually sing along rather than just making corresponding noises. Music is unique as a language learning tool in that the writers tend to seek out poetic vocabulary. This provides you with a unique opportunity in that you will be able to develop your language skills while laying a strong foundation of vocabulary words.

Adding lyric videos into your comprehensible input is powerful for a couple of reasons. First off, if you are going to sing along with a song you should know what you are saying. The last thing you want is to sing perfectly in time with a popular song only to have someone ask you what it means when you do not know. Verifying you are really understanding your listening comprehension practice is a fantastic way to go about self evaluation. Most importantly, though, you are going to have the advantage of learning a new language by listening to music. A secondary advantage to adding lyric videos to your second language strategies toolkit is the vocabulary words you will have access to when you do. Artists are always trying to find the **best** way to say things. Choosing music as a place to lay your foundation is beneficial for that reason as well. Of course, you will always have the opportunity to bond with people over the music you enjoy. Aside from access to unique new words, you will be faced with different tempos and ways of pronouncing things.

In order to get some things to rhyme, musicians will often play with the way they pronounce different words. Once you see how many ways there are to pronounce words in your target language you can worry less about speaking perfectly. There is a proper way to pronounce words, but if you are being understood when you speak then it really does not matter. This is important because in any language there are a myriad of ways to pronounce different words. Just in English you can read potato or potato or tomato or tomato or read or read or lead or lead or record or record or object or object and so on and so on. Yes, changing the pronunciation can change the meaning, but more often than not the context is more important than the pronunciation. That is where grammar rules come into play. Fortunately for people like me, grammar is secondary to vocabulary when it comes to songwriting. In other words, you are going to need to supplement music lyric videos with grammar work.

Perhaps the best part of using music as comprehensible input is that you can use it passively. You will have plenty of time to listen to music throughout your day. Whether you are listening to it at the gym, in the car, or around the house, just having music on is going to help you with your second language acquisition. The more time you spend around the language the better, foreign languages are fun like that. Irrespective of your learning style, being able to collect fun wins is important and music allows for that.

Catching a new word or several new words when you are listening to music is an incredible feeling. These are wins you can start stacking immediately. While you can certainly do this with audiobooks and podcasts, music tends to be more enjoyable. Cutting up a 3-5 minute piece is easier and more consumable than something that is several hours long. Every time you recognize a new word you take another step towards fluency. That in and of itself should provide you with ample motivation when you feel you have hit a wall.

     Working on your language skills is going to take time, so it is imperative that you do what you can to avoid boredom. Music is perhaps the best solution for avoiding boredom. With how many genres of music there are, you can jump around and find new and exciting music wherever you go. It would be wrong of me to go all this time speaking only about listening comprehension, though. Listening to music is fantastic, but you need to be writing if you want things to stick. That is where the next level of language learning strategies comes into play.

     As mentioned above, there are levels to your immersion environment. Adding passive input first simply ensures you have ample exposure to the language. Next, is finding ways to turn your passive input into active input. At the end of the day, you need both. That is where this next exercise comes into play. The worst activity of all language learning (perhaps an exaggeration, perhaps not) is dictation. An average language learner is likely not going to do this. Listening to things and writing down what you *think* you hear is not an enjoyable activity. Mostly because you will be forced to see just how far you have yet to go. On the other hand, you will find that your language skills develop at a quicker rate when you do difficult things. Training your ear is difficult, you cannot simply do it passively, as great as that would be.

     Listen to songs, even songs you have heard dozens of times, and write down what you think you are hearing. Then, check your work.Once you have written down what you think you heard, it is time to check your work. Whether you have the lyrics up on a website or the lyric video up on YouTube is irrelevant, all you need to do is double check yourself. The easiest way to do this is to play the lyric video and write rather than read. Every 30 seconds pause it and check your work. Do this with 2-3 songs every day and you will be astonished at what you learn. That will be 20 dictation exercises all while listening to music you enjoy and learning what it is about and what you are saying when you sing along. After you master a few dozen songs, try to expand into art outside of music.

  Poetry, short stories, audiobooks, podcasts, documentaries, all of these things and more are available to you in audio format. These days it is rare to find media that does **not** offer translation and transcription to at least some extent. In fact, you could even turn the television on and play something in your target language then write what you are hearing and verify how much you got right. Using these forms of art to learn a new language may also prompt you to practice by beginning to make some art of your own. Consuming various forms of comprehensible input is great, but you should be creating just as much as you are consuming. If you want to learn to speak you need to learn to think and creating is precisely how you do that. Not only that, by writing and creating you are going to come face to face with keywords you need to know. It will be difficult to do this in a new language if you have never done it in your first language, but it is far from impossible. You do not, however, need to spend all of your time searching through YouTube. Often some of the best options are found on smaller websites that have not tried to break into YouTube yet.

  When I was traveling abroad, I probably toured 30 museums, 100 churches, and many, many other culturally significant places from battlefields to riverways. The best part about tours, whether they be a museum or a memorial site, they usually are offered in multiple languages. Not just that, but choosing your target language rather than your native language is free. When I first started with it I realized that it would be a great way to understand the local language while also being able to hear a native speaker, or native speakers, discuss things that were important to the country I was living in at the time. Tours give you the opportunity to connect with the local culture while simultaneously using that information as a resource to bolster your language learning.

      Because most of the tours are now digital, you have a unique opportunity to take advantage of this access to native speakers. If they are live classes, even better. That means you can ask questions and practice words, grammar, and speaking yourself. Learning through context clues and hints that are given by the exhibits (and the explanations that are also written in English) can make the experience that much more enjoyable. However, it is easy to default out when doing tours like this, so try to remain engaged as much as possible without reverting back to the language with which you are the most comfortable.One of the easiest ways to create a connection with a native speaker is to ask them questions about things they enjoy. If someone is giving a tour, asking them questions about the material, irrespective of what it is, will be beneficial. It will get you to speak, you will have someone personally teach you, and you will have fun doing it. Sure, the first time it is a daunting task, but every time you do something difficult it gets easier. Sharing the fact that you are working on your language learning will also likely have an effect on how the tour is treated. You may get special information you may not have otherwise received, you may make more friends, you may just get to speak more.

      In line with asking questions is being well informed. You should ask questions, yes, but you also need to be informed so that you are not asking about things that have already been covered. Reading everything will help you avoid this when talking to native speakers. For the most part, all of the information you are going to need is written, in your native language, somewhere in the place you are touring. From that information you can develop new questions and, possibly, even become a resource to other language learners around you. Free online courses are great and can help a lot, but there is little that can replace the on the ground experience of speaking to a native speaker that is completely free as well.With all that said, there is something about these tours that I think is overlooked and it is really important. Tours are a time to focus on the things you are already interested in because, as stated above, focusing on what you are interested in makes language learning more sustainable.

    One of the aspects that is most important to language learning is memory encoding. The long and short of it is that the more senses that are stimulated when a memory is created, the stronger that memory is and will be. That is why certain smells or sounds can often trigger feelings of nostalgia. The way we leverage this as language learners is by ensuring that every time we are working on our target language we are also incorporating additional senses. Listening to music and reading lyrics. Speaking while out on a walk in nature where you don't have to be afraid to make mistakes. Asking questions to native speakers during a museum tour in your hometown or in a foreign country with your family. All of these things add additional stimulus that helps with memory encoding and can pay off in the short and long term for anyone studying a new language. Using the language in the real world and in day to day life is important, but can be difficult to simulate online. Not just that, but real world experience allows you to develop mnemonics that you would not have otherwise thought of had you stuck exclusively to language apps and flash cards.

    I recommend checking out places around you that offer tours. The best part about museums is that even in English speaking countries they always have bilinguals and audio available in several languages, one of which is hopefully your target language. So if you are struggling to find a way to get real practice, look for some places that offer tours near you and see which languages they are offered in, you might just get lucky and make a new local friend to practice with, or better yet a resource for your family moving forward. Whether it's churches, old towns, history museums, art museums, or anything else, it is worth making the effort to see what is out there.

The Penultimate Step

The final step to your Localized Immersion is going to be adding in your own creations. At the end of the day your goal should be to **think** in your target language. That means you are going to have to begin creating at one point or another. Translation, reading aloud, listening to music, watching movies, all of that is consumption. If all you do is consume, all you **will be able to do is consume.** Whether you like it or not, speaking a second language involves creating in that language. Fortunately, all you need to do is start creating; and you can begin at any time. In fact, I would encourage you to start creating in your target language long before you ever feel comfortable speaking it. From the very start you should be writing and doing everything in your power to create a written record. This will serve you for months, even years, into your second language acquisition.

In steps it looks like this:

First:
- Find Music
- Listen to Music

Second
- Write Things Down (Dictation)
- Check Your Work

Third
- Make Your Own Art
- Constant Reiterations

Fourth
- Immerse your mind
- Learn to **think** in your target language

Creating your own art is terrifying. However, if you are doing it in a new language you have an excuse *if* it is less than satisfactory. When your language skills are in their infantile state, making mistakes is common. Making sense is often rare. But if you focus on your language output being artistic you will be forced to hone your communication skills. Does your speech all have to be eloquent and melodic? Absolutely not. You should be working to get to that point, though.Making art will necessarily involve writing. Written language operates differently than spoken language because grammar structures and spelling become highly important. When speaking these things can quickly become irrelevant, but not when writing. That is why you need to be writing down potential ideas. Not only that, but as you write different ideas down you will find that you are more inspired than before. Thought inspires deeper thought. Take advantage of this when working to develop new skills in your target language.

As you are writing your own ideas down, be sure to ask people for other ideas. In any of the world languages there are endless approaches to art. If you are feeling stagnant or unable to come up with ideas, asking people to share their ideas is perfect. You will not always like the idea, but you may find that the idea you did not like spurred a new one that you *do* like. However, the more you write the more time you need to dedicate to going back and checking your previous work. Making corrections on sentences and phrases you came up with will allow you to become more precise and eloquent in your speech.

As standards have fallen the ability to write has become more and more rare. Being able to write is being able to think and the better you write the easier it will be for you to think. There is a reason that writing things down will help you remember them whether you are writing down the tasks you need to accomplish or you are writing down new words you are learning. Not only does it help with your memory, but it helps with your thought process. Often when people are faced with a problem they do what they can to think it through in their head. This rarely works, however, because it is rather difficult to remember your train of thought as you get further into the self discussion. By writing these things down not only will you get it out of your head, which may result in you not feeling the need to worry about it anymore, you will also be able to reason through the thought in a more thorough way. While this is to your benefit within your native language, it will also enhance and accelerate your second language acquisition.

     Fortunately, when it comes to writing, there are many different approaches which means you do not have to spend hours forcing yourself to do something you dislike. Most people spend their time writing essays in school, and while this can be beneficial in helping understand and demonstrate an understanding of the covered material, it is often tedious and even boring.

Now that you are in control of your education, you get to decide what you want to spend your time doing. If you like to write poetry, write poetry in your target language. If you like to write short stories, write short stories to develop your language skills. On the other hand, if you are one of the people, like myself, who enjoyed writing essays after reading, then do that!

     Irrespective of what you are writing, the fact you are writing is what matters most. The problem with many language teachers is that they end up having their students focus on the things the teachers find important. While standardized tests are useful in ensuring the school continues to get paid, they are rarely a quality measurement of proficiency. This is why keeping a written record from early on is so important. When you are writing in month 5 you will be happy to go back and look at how far you've come from only being able to string together three sentences. Without tracking your numbers it can feel as though you have not made any progress. There are already so many things fighting against you, do not add another one when you have complete control over it. Write early and often and keep your notebooks so you can always go back to correct, iterate, and remember just how much work you have put in to get to where you are.

Another form of writing that many do not consider when embarking on this adventure is journaling. Whether you call it a diary, a journal, or something else, maintaining a written record of your day is often worthwhile. However, being able to do so in your target language comes with a few unique benefits. For one you will be forced to think through your day and recite it on paper. Thinking in your target language is the goal, after all, and by writing about your day you will force yourself to think in your target language in the same way you think in your native language. The benefits of this are numerous, but the greatest benefit is that it will be easier for you to recall the words that correspond with your everyday vocabulary.

At the end of the day, you will speak in your second language the same way you speak in your first language. If you wait to learn how to speak the way you naturally speak, you will delay your escape from the Silent Period and the fear of speaking will likely increase with time. We will discuss more about the Silent Period and how you can escape it in the next chapter, but for now I want to discuss the levels you should be seeking to achieve throughout your implementation of Localized Immersion.

Levels to This Thing

There are two different arenas we are going to focus on when it comes to leveling up your Localized Immersion. The first is going to be difficulty levels. When it comes to comprehensible input you are finding online, there are several steps you can take to modify the difficulty. Subtitles are probably the most prolific and you will be able to use them for months on end to continue progressing at an acceptable rate. Starting out try to have the audio in your target language with the subtitles in your target language.

If that's too much, follow this progression:

1. **Subtitles in target language, audio in native language**
2. **Subtitles in native language, audio in target language**
3. **Subtitles and audio in target language**
4. **Audio only in target language**

    Whether it takes you one month or one year to work through this progression is irrelevant. So long as you are making consistent strides in your comprehension of different vocabulary words and grammar structures, you are moving in the right direction. Some people will spend a week on the first two and half of a year on the third step. Few people will skip step one and proceed quickly to step four. Most people will spend a month on step one, two months on step two, three months on step three, and four months on step four. Learning a language does not have to take years, but the process also does not happen overnight. Remember that when you are feeling as though you are falling behind; and pull out your trusty notebook so you can get a glimpse at where you were to put into perspective where you currently are.

    While you have the notebook out, it is time to dive into the iterative phase. That is to say, the phase when you push to improve your vocabulary and the structures of your sentences. At first you will have a dictionary, but when you are working on iterations you are going to work better with a thesaurus. There are websites like reverso.com that will help you with synonyms, conjugations, and sentence structure. The first time you write a story out it will more than likely be riddled with mistakes. Some big, some massive. This is only a problem if you plan to walk away and never look back. While that is certainly an option, if you are taking your second language acquisition seriously you will need to avoid it. Much of your progress will come during the iterative process. Whether you go back daily, weekly, or monthly, the process is the same.

Here is what it looks like step by step:

1. **Create the content**
2. **Step away to consume some content**
3. **Return to the original content with more knowledge than you had when you created it**
4. **Make corrections to your vocabulary, syntax, grammar, and rewrite the content**
5. **Repeat steps 2-4 until you are satisfied by the precision and flow**

Seems simple, right? That's because it is simple. Unfortunately, simple and easy are not the same thing. This might end up being one of the most challenging activities you do when you are working on your second language. However, because it is so challenging it will also be a place where you start *thinking* in your target language here. It is all but required if you plan to accurately portray yourself in a story. The first time you might feel frustrated, but push through that and find out what is on the other side of the language barrier.

Keep in mind, very few people are capable of telling a story perfectly the first time. Even in their native language. Rather than trying to tell the perfect story, try telling the most detailed story. Over time this will evolve into the perfect story and you will be able to recall more details the next time you go to talk about something else. That is perhaps one of the greatest side effects of this sort of exercise. When you try to recall something once you will remember a certain amount, let's say 50%. Every time you go back and try to recall more, during the iterative process for example, you will add say 5% to your recollection. Details, names, places, all of it will come rushing back to you over time. But there is one more layer you need to add in order to get the most out of this work you are doing.

I often discuss how important it is to create more than you consume. Comprehensible input is important, but that does not mean you should spend years just training your listening skills. Speaking foreign languages *is* creating in foreign languages. The same is true for writing. Every time you sit down with a pen and paper and work on your written language you are actively creating in a new language. Knowing that, there are ways to turn your own creations into your study materials. Obviously you do not have to do this with everything all the time, but if you do it even 25% of the time you will enhance and accelerate your second language acquisition. The easiest way to do this is using the very same stories you created. Simply start reading them aloud. Reading something aloud is unique, especially when it is your own creation. Even in your first language you might find that the way you write and the way you speak vary drastically. While you will eventually want to bring these two things closer together, everyone starts somewhere. Here are some things you should be asking yourself as you read your stories aloud:

1. Does it sound right?

2. Is it complete?

3. How can you make it better?

Working through these questions will help you keep your momentum going even when you feel like things are beginning to slow down. Once you are satisfied with where you are at there is one final step to storytelling. Turning it into a bigger story. You do not have to share these if you do not want to, but knowing the language that goes into embellishment, exaggeration, and hyperbole will help you when you are speaking to native speakers. Not only that, but knowing how to exaggerate and embellish will also make the time you spend listening to and reading your second language more meaningful.

As standards have fallen the ability to write has become more and more rare. Unfortunately this is to the detriment of more than just the public education system. Being able to write is being able to think and the better you write the easier it will be for you to think. There is a reason that writing things down will help you remember them whether you are writing down the tasks you need to accomplish or you are writing down new words you are learning. Not only does it help with your memory, but it helps with your thought process. Often when people are faced with a problem they do what they can to think it through in their head. This rarely works, however, because it is rather difficult to remember your train of thought as you get further into the self discussion. By writing these things down not only will you get it out of your head, which may result in you not feeling the need to worry about it anymore, you will also be able to reason through the thought in a more thorough way. While this is to your benefit within your native language, it will also enhance and accelerate your second language acquisition. Fortunately, when it comes to writing, there are many different approaches which means you do not have to spend hours forcing yourself to do something you dislike. Most people spend their time writing essays in school, and while this can be beneficial in helping understand and demonstrate an understanding of the covered material, it is often tedious and even boring.

Now that you are in control of your education, you get to decide what you want to spend your time doing. If you like to write poetry, write poetry in your target language. If you like to write short stories, write short stories to develop your language skills. On the other hand, if you are one of the people, like myself, who enjoyed writing essays after reading, then do that! Irrespective of what you are writing, the fact you are writing is what matters most. The problem with many language teachers is that they end up having their students focus on the things the teachers find important. While standardized tests are useful in ensuring the school continues to get paid, they are rarely a quality measurement of proficiency. That is why many native speakers often find themselves failing language classes that are being given in their native language. It is rare that someone understands to a high degree the grammar rules of their mother tongue. So while you can certainly approach language learning in the same way the public education system does, if you do you may find yourself bored, discouraged, or worse.

The last form of writing that many do not consider when embarking on this adventure is journaling. Whether you call it a diary, a journal, or something else, maintaining a written record of your day is often worthwhile. However, being able to do so in your target language comes with a few unique benefits. For one you will be forced to think through your day and recite it on paper. Thinking in your target language is the goal, after all, and by writing about your day you will force yourself to think in your target language in the same way you think in your native language. The benefits of this are numerous, but the greatest benefit is that it will be easier for you to recall the words that correspond with your everyday vocabulary.

Add this portion into the iterative process and watch as much of what confused you begins to make sense. It is incredible how much of the content you consume is exaggerated to some extent and having a grasp of the terms used in conjunction with different grammar structures will take your overall comprehension to the next level.
The more you use it, the easier it will be to spot in the wild. Kind of like that feeling where you learn a new word or concept and suddenly begin seeing it everywhere. It will happen in your second language just as often as it happens in your first language. It can be dangerous to rely on your memory for second language acquisition, but if you do it right you might find it is the perfect tool to take your language skills to the next level.

Whether you like it or not, telling stories is human nature and even if you decide to never tell yours, other people will tell you theirs. Learning the language people use to express themselves and tell stories is absolutely crucial if you plan to speak with native speakers in a foreign country. If you are learning a language, that should be your minimum goal in my humble opinion. Creating is more difficult than consuming. This is a universal truth and nothing above is going to be easy, irrespective of how simple the task is. If you can push yourself to the point where you are creating at least a quarter of the time you are studying, you will be shocked at how quickly you progress. It will be difficult, but you can do difficult things and be great. Remember to record your stories for posterity's sake, because, at the end of the day, when there are emotions tied to your memories they are easier to recall; irrespective of the language in which you made the memories.

Making memories with emotions

After working with hundreds of students over the past year, one thing about the education they seem to have received stood out above the rest. Whether they had been out of school for 1 year or 25 years, everyone had a good grasp of the basics. They knew the alphabet, they could recite it with some guidance and they knew a fair few words. Grammar structures were still difficult, but even present tense conjugation returned with only a few exercises. Even irregularities were recalled frequently. Drilling the basics is important. There is no argument about that. The problem comes in that the basics are all the students ever had the chance to experience. While there are certainly students who avoided putting the work in when they were young, there are also students who worked hard and learned what they could and still they have a huge gap in their knowledge. Up to four years learning a new language and only ever seeing three or four verb tenses is embarrassing.

That is what the standardized tests require you to know, though. So that is what the teachers focus on to keep their jobs. Some will challenge you, but many are trying to ensure everyone hits the minimum standard. This is a noble endeavor, unfortunately it is often at the expense of the students who excel in class. For that reason, for better or worse, everyone I have worked with knows the basics well and is eager to learn new concepts. They were always only missing one component: Progressive Overload. When you spend years on end working on the same concepts over and over again you are going to be able to remember them. Years later, when you haven't even thought about your second language classes in years, you will be able to remember certain things simply because you were confronted with them so often in class.

      That is why many Spanish students know how to ask where certain things are, how much things cost, and several greetings and salutations. Often they can count, name colors, talk about shapes and animals, but they cannot conjugate for the past tense or future tense.

      The negatives here are self evident, but there is a silver lining if you are willing to take it. Even if all you remember are words and one conjugation, you still know those things and already have a head start on the foundation you will need to build. That is where the concept of Language Recovery comes from. Precisely because you have so much latent knowledge. There is rarely a reason to start your second language acquisition at zero and if you have any history with a language you will be able to build a system where it does not feel as if you are starting from zero. Foreign languages are all around you whether you realize it or not. From signs to menus to popular music, knowing a second language will reveal to you just how many opportunities you have to work on your target language in your day to day life.

      You already know that you don't have to start from zero, but you should also be adding any new words you see into your working memory. Pay attention to your surroundings and watch as your progress just how many new vocabulary words you come across. Again, just in a restaurant you will inevitably come across dozens of words you can focus on learning like, agua, fresca, huevos, desayuno, almuerzo, cena, lengua, cabeza, ajo, papas, dorado, vegetariana, molida, frijoles, and more.

Using opportunities like this to increase your second language competency is a low barrier to entry and directly useful and productive language that you are adding to your repertoire. When you are looking at other menus in other languages try to think of how you would go about translating dish descriptions.

Think about how they might be named in your target language. This is just one way to up your language output and put some holes in the language barrier in front of you. The final step in the process is saying all of these things out loud so that you can practice spoken word simultaneously. Working with menus is important because it gives you an opportunity to construct some sentence frames. By focusing on productive language that you know for a fact you will use when face to face with native speakers you give yourself a little breathing room you would not otherwise have. Learning a foreign language is going to require language output. The closer you can get to an immersion environment the better. Adding in little exercises like this will allow you to build that learning environment without becoming overwhelmed.

What you will notice is that the things you remember are things that left an impression, one way or the other. Often it is a phrase or a word that makes you laugh and the memory of laughing along with this phrase makes it easier to recall the phrase itself. This is something you can use to your advantage when you are going through the learning process.

Try to tie the new vocabulary words you are learning into an emotional memory. Telling jokes is a fantastic way to start. Work on your listening skills by watching comedies. Subtitles might help, but wordplay is vital for many comedians. All that means is that over time you will have the opportunity to understand the comedy specials on deeper and deeper levels. The same is true in your first language.

Odds are, in your favorite comedy special, movie, or TV show, you missed something the first time through that was a pleasure to catch the next time you watched it.

In your second language you will be able to watch the same thing 3 or 4 times without getting tired of it because you will probably find something new each time. You shouldn't necessarily do this back to back, maybe once per week or once every other week, but give it a shot. Write down the words you hear and don't recognize, make notes of the time stamps for jokes you *do* understand so you know what to expect the next time through. Then go about your normal study routine, listening to various inputs, reading, writing, and speaking when you get the chance.

Chances are you will shock yourself with what you are able to do the next time you listen to the comedy special.Make jokes with the words you are learning. The connections across languages can be hilarious, and laughing at them **will help you remember.** Again, the emotion does not have to be laughter. You can write short stories to express whatever it is you are feeling. So long as you are tying some emotion to the word, and writing down what you can, you will have the best chance at recalling what you are learning. Once you have surrounded yourself with the new language, it's time to add in one final piece.

The Final Step: There is no escape

People have been debating whether or not it is possible to really *think* in a new language. The view around here is, of course, not only can you think in a new language, if you truly want to be bilingual you must think in a new language. While there are several approaches to getting to that point, there is one thing that works better than most others. This is where mainstream classrooms let their students down. Best case scenario in the public education industry you learn how to memorize and regurgitate phrases or translate sentences directly indefinitely. Translating your thoughts is good, but it does not have to be the final step. The perfect way to train yourself to think in your target language is by playing mental chess. Some people might call this something else, but I like the term mental chess because that is really what you are doing. Playing out conversations in your head, in advance, complete with multiple hypothetical responses. Here is what it looks like in steps:

1. Write down three conversations you have recently had

You can do as few or as many as you want, but the important thing is having more than one to work with so you can jump around when you hit a stopping point. Writing these down is paramount because you will be working through them multiple times in your second language. Precision is going to be important, but everyone starts somewhere. Nothing will be perfect the first time, so write it down and just get started.

2. Translate them word for word

Next you are going to take what you wrote and translate it all word for word. If you are able to do more than translate it word for word, then do it. However, if direct translation is what you have to do, then start there. Bust open your bilingual dictionary and take as long as you must to get the conversation translated into your target language. When you are doing this write the sentence out in your native language first then immediately beneath it write it down in your new language. Do this for the whole conversation.

3. Write it all down

Self explanatory on this one. Just keep a log in written language. Keeping a language learning journal as you go through all of your second language acquisition will change your experience in ways you cannot imagine. Language output is just as if not more important than comprehensible input and, in a way, this exercise is you creating your own comprehensible input. The best of both worlds.

4. Run through hypotheticals

Now the time for mental chess comes in and the hard work begins. Ideally you will end up with a web of potential conversations that you can follow endlessly. Take this opportunity to practice your proficiency with grammar structures and learn some new vocabulary words. Keep in mind that written language and spoken language are often different, but do not let this stop you from making progress. One way or another you are going to work through these conversations and as you begin to speak them aloud you will find new and better ways to speak.

5. Work out how to say it better

As a final step, you are going to work through several iterations. This is not something you are going to be doing immediately. Set time aside each week for this and go back to attack one conversation. Look at how you worded things, look at it in your native language and make any corrections or improvements you can. Then look at how you translated it.

Make all of the corrections you can and push yourself to improve the wording. Strive for precision and eloquence. Having all of these things written down is useful for reasons beyond simple memory encoding. Yes, your short term memory and long term memory will benefit from the writing, but you will also see that there are more benefits to your foreign language skills. Writing and speaking are closely related, particularly when you are working on conversations you know you have had or will have in the future. Thinking ahead in this way is beneficial and, while it does involve writing, the next step does not.

Assuming you have been writing all of these conversations down, your next step is perfecting your accent. Practicing fluidity will give you confidence when it comes time to test your metal with native speakers. Read everything aloud and pay close attention to how it feels. You might occasionally have the feeling that something you wrote doesn't translate quite right and there might be a better way to say it.

Follow that intuition. Fortunately, there is a way to build that intuition and it's pretty simple. Start translating all of your conversations and thoughts in real time. At first you might struggle, but over time this activity gets to be pretty enjoyable. You don't have to do it all the time, but the more you try the quicker your language skills will develop. Make mental notes of the words you get stuck on and if possible right them down for a future study session. Doing this is crucial because you are learning to speak your second language in the same way you speak your first language. Mastering the words you use habitually will increase your confidence in speaking generally.

Once you get used to doing those things, adding a thesaurus to the mix will take your second language acquisition to the next level. Not only will you diversify your vocabulary in your new language, you will likely encounter some new vocabulary words in your native language. Finding ways to use these new found words will challenge you, but if you continue writing them down and working them into your conversations they will stick. The primary issue with this method is that you will find yourself lost in thought more and more often and in more than one language. At its worst you may find yourself unable to answer questions in day to day conversations because you are translating everything unnecessarily.

Try to avoid this and stick to translating conversations when you are **not** in the middle of them. Going through the conversations and hypothetical responses may be considered "over thinking" by some people, but in the context of second language acquisition it is different. Essentially, the theory is that you will play how you practice. If you never practice the words you are going to use in conversations, the way you have used them in hundreds of conversations before then you are going to struggle in basic conversations. Not being able to express yourself during routine conversations can be devastating to one's confidence.

Eventually your goal is to be thinking in the new language entirely. The best part about this method is that it really does not *feel* like studying because you aren't looking things up, you don't have to worry about making mistakes because it's all in your head, and you have endless opportunities throughout the day to try. Over time you will improve, but forcing yourself to think in your second language is exhausting. Whenever you feel like you are getting burnt out, take a moment away from it. You will be amazed at how much more you understand when you return to your second language acquisition after a time away. Focus on incremental improvements. One sentence, then two, then three, until you find yourself drifting away in thought.

Learning to think in a new language is absolutely necessary and it is incredible to me that people think you can learn a new language and speak it fluently while constantly translating every single word in and out. Your end goal should be for your language output to be equally as fluid in both your first and second language. For that to happen you **must** think in the new language. It will take time and there is no easy way, but the more you do it the quicker the transition will happen. While it is nearly impossible to say at what point the switch will flip, it will at one point and when it does you will know. Suddenly you will no longer see things as they are called in your native language, you will see them as they are called in your target language. Rather than thinking about how you will introduce yourself to a stranger in your native language, you will think about how you will do it in your second language. Everything will change and you might find yourself struggling to remember words in your native language rather than the new one.

Part of learning to think in your target language is learning to approach different problems from different angles. When you have more tools in your belt you have more ways to tackle each new obstacle you encounter. Polysemy is a powerful tool that will enhance and accelerate your second language acquisition.Learning to express yourself in different contexts is one of the most important skills you can develop because these are the moments when direct translation will fail you most. Making mistakes is part of the game, but if you practice speaking in different contexts you will spend less time making big mistakes. In line with creative thinking, to develop these complete sentences yourself, you should be getting as much exposure to your new language as possible.

When you are working on your listening skills, try to find times when the orators are using the same word to express different things. Your speaking ability will increase the more often you are exposed to the language and listening to native speakers is necessary. In large part because they will open your eyes to different ways you should be saying things to sound more natural. Doing this and translating your own sentences will set you up for success in ways most other methods simply cannot.

Get to the point where you associate the word with specific situations. That is why writing stories, or journal entries, is such an incredible exercise. You are challenging yourself to think about things and put words to them in the language you are learning. In essence, you are achieving our goal of **thinking** in your second language. So read your sentences aloud and see how they flow together. Once you can read one, try two, then three, and so on. Remember, just because you would have said or always said something the same way does not mean that it will make sense in your second language. Sometimes things just do not make sense and the difficulty many language learners face is learning to accept that. At the end of the day, there are aspects of languages that simply are because they are.

The English language is a prime example of this, and while there are explanations for many things, the fact remains that some things simply are because they are. There will be times when you find yourself asking, "why do they say it like that?" and the honest answer is, "because they do" and because they do you must learn to as well. This is what makes being a translator so difficult and why I always recommend translating to at least some extent when you are working on your language skills. You will find that you learn not only new ways to express yourself in your second language, but some potential ways to express yourself in your native language, too. The final key is developing and maximizing your pattern recognition.

Pattern Recognition

When it comes to language learning strategies, one of the most important things to focus on is how many points of reference a given word has for you. If you understand the etymology of the words, then you are more likely to remember the word. People often spend hours upon hours looking up words they have already searched for and it is because they lack a frame of reference. For those who spend most of their time searching up words on their phone, you may find that the words simply are not sticking and that is happening for the same reason that phones and tablets and televisions never seem to make their way into your dreams.

    The best place to place emphasis when it comes to pattern recognition in foreign languages is within language families. Etymology can be useful, but often it becomes irrelevant depending on your target language. If you are learning a second romance language, etymology will likely help you, but if not there is more value in focusing on only the words you are learning and where they originate. You want to focus on the things that are most useful to you and of all the things you can focus on, your main objective should be understanding the language you use on a consistent basis. Language families are an important part of language learning because they can be used to rapidly expand your competency without too much effort. The reason for this is there are consistent patterns that exist within every language family and often these patterns are more important to learn than individual vocabulary words or grammar rules. This is especially true if you are working on a language that is within the same language family as your mother tongue, or even your second language. While patterns exist across all languages, those that exist within the same language family can be used to enhance and accelerate progress to a high degree.

The a few examples of language families are:
- Romance
- Germanic
- Indo-European
- Sino-Tibetan
- Creole
- Afro-Asiatic

For this book we will focus primarily on the romance language family. Depending on the foreign language you are targeting, some self evaluation through the patterns of your target language may be useful. Whether it is finding key words, learning the correct usage of different grammar concepts, or focusing on listening comprehension across languages, understanding the basic language family will pay off in the short and long term. Comprehensible input is great, but many teachers miss out on the opportunity to provide students with a more holistic view of language. Developing language skills is far easier when you are able to see more than just words when you are studying. One of the greatest tools you have in your language learning journey is going to be your vocabulary in your first language. Every time you learn a new word you give yourself an advantage in your target language because it is possible that the new language you learn will coincide with words in your target language.

      Most people avoid working on their first language because they assume they do not need to expand their competency. This could not be further from the truth. In fact, one of the most detrimental things for language learning is believing that you need to be able to understand 100% of something you are reading. Generally, people will stop their first language acquisition when they reach fluency, that is why there is such a focus in schools on maintaining some form of growth throughout primary and secondary education. However, pursuing a larger vocabulary outside the classroom has its benefits and they extend far beyond the ability to speak more eloquently in your native language.

There are many words that come from an ancient language base and expanding beyond the contemporary will give you a glimpse into the roots of the words you are learning in your target language. In short, by learning words in your native language that many people no longer use or that sound as if they are outdated, you will likely be learning the words in multiple languages. Here are just a few examples:

to write = scribe = escribir (Spanish)

vent = window = ventana (Spanish)

free = liberty = libre (Spanish)

acknowledge/admit = avow = avouer (French)

explain = explicate = explicar (Spanish) = expliquer (French)

understand = comprehend = comprender (Spanish) = comprendre (French)

finish = terminate = terminar (Spanish) = terminer (French)

As you can see, one of the aspects that many language teachers neglect is how to think of, and in, other languages. Whether it's your first language, second language, third, or fourth, by teaching yourself to think *differently* you will find that you are able to understand other languages more easily. While this language "hack" will not work every time, you will be surprised at how often you see words you know in words you are learning when you are actively looking for it. Aside from the patterns you will encounter within the vocabulary across languages, you will also find there are patterns across the grammar rules.

If you are able to speak fluently and with as few mistakes as possible, you will find that you are willing to speak more often. Confidence is key when it comes to speaking fluidly because, at one point or another, you will realize that it does not matter whether or not you make mistakes. As a master musician knows, the only time people will realize that you made a mistake is when you slow down and acknowledge it yourself. When you spend time memorizing grammar rules, you may find yourself paralyzed by fear when you are unable to recall the precise configuration of the sentence you are trying to construct. Grammar is important, there are patterns to be found there, but do not let imperfection deter you from speaking. The only way to get better is to do it. The only way to master anything is to risk being bad at it. No one is perfect or even good when they start, but so long as you start fluency is a near guarantee.

Part of finding patterns is looking for them. This is something that most people do not think to do, especially as they are learning languages. You should always be questioning the things you are seeing and asking yourself if there are patterns that lie within them. When you are looking for patterns you are far more likely to find them. The average language learner neglects this portion of language learning, usually to their own detriment. Using this tool will not only sharpen it, but it will enhance and accelerate your second language acquisition, and it will carry over into every other language you choose to learn. That said, many of the grammar rules you encounter that do have patterns to them will be within the same language family. If you are struggling to find similarities, though it may be worthwhile taking time to think about the similarities *within* the differences.

Patterns are not always the things that are the same, often you will find them lying within the things that differentiate. The development of your language skills does not stop at recognition of the alike. Every foreign language is tied together in different ways and the more you look for these ties the easier it will be for you to see them. Whether you choose to look for patterns in the vocabulary, in the grammar, or somewhere else so long as you are looking for them it will be beneficial. When you are working within the same language family you will certainly discover more than if you are jumping around from one language to another, but irrespective of which language you are learning there will be overlaps. You can find them by diving deeper into your native language and expanding your vocabulary. You can find them by learning and mastering the grammar rules of your native language. However you choose to do it, all that matters is that you do choose to look.

After you spend several months working on your language skills you may begin to feel as though things are becoming too routine. If you are not constantly expanding as a language learner you may find yourself frustrated. This is a normal step in the process, but giving up on your target language is simply not an option. Any time you are learning a new language, sometimes the best thing you can do is return to the things you already know. The ability to spot patterns in your work can save you plenty of time, but more importantly they can turn boring activities into something more enjoyable. When you take time to actively develop your language skills you will not only improve in your first language, but in your new language as well.

Repetition is absolutely necessary for success in language learning. Duolingo takes this to the extreme which, at a certain point, becomes counterproductive. Doing things time and time again and improving with every repetition will accelerate and enhance your second language acquisition. However, when your sole focus is repetition you will get bored. Of course there are times when you are going to do things you do not enjoy, but if you spend too much time feeling like your time is being wasted you will likely give up on your language learning goals.

Ensuring you have ample content and a diverse set of resources to sort through will help as you can focus on vocabulary words and grammar rules in different contexts. Whereas if you spend all of your time reading, writing from the same person or listening to the same orator you will make progress. That said, you will also find that you end up using the same vocabulary words and the same grammar structure over and over and over again. It will be difficult to expand into different areas, listen to orators who speak at different speeds, and read things you do not entirely understand, it will be worthwhile.

    At the beginning of your language learning journey you are likely going to spend far more time with your first language than with your target language. Learning a new language is far easier if you have a good grasp of your mother tongue. By learning the patterns that correlate with your native language you may just stumble across patterns in your new language. Writing is one of the best ways to get this process started. Placing an emphasis on patterns will allow you to see them more often and with more ease both in your first and second languages.

    The first place to start is with writing sentences and doing what you can to track down the grammar patterns. If you know that in English you can change most adjectives to adverbs by adding an -ly to the end, then maybe there is a suffix that corresponds in your target language. If you know that adding -ed to a verb makes it past tense then perhaps there is a corresponding pattern in your target language. Whatever it may be, when you actively pay attention to the sentences you are writing and how words interact in different contexts you will begin seeing patterns. Once you are beginning to see patterns you can look for example after example and write them down. As per usual, if you do not write down the things you find you will have a difficult time recalling them when it is time to speak.

    At the same time, every pattern you find in the new language you are learning is one you should look for within your first language. While doing this will certainly help you in your reading comprehension, you will also be surprised how much more simple speaking becomes. Knowing patterns will ensure you spend less time thinking and more time doing which is what normally holds people back. There are many pieces to fluency, but the ability to speak fluidly is paramount. It does not have to be perfect, but it does need to be fluid. Above all, though, do not limit your time seeking patterns to only your language learning. Patterns are everywhere and while it is fantastic to see them in languages, the more you see them in the world around you the more this skill will serve you in other areas of your life.

Looking for patterns in everything you do is difficult, but the more you do it the easier it will be. There will also be times when you see patterns that no one else does. When this happens do your best to follow it as much as possible. Just because other people are not seeing the same patterns does not mean they will not be useful to you. The reason we shared the pattern guides in this article is to give you the jumpstart you need to start seeing them everywhere. Pattern recognition is a skill, like language learning, and it must be actively developed. Fortunately, if you develop this skill outside of your language learning you will be able to transfer that ability into your language learning. Expanding your knowledge of the world will enhance and accelerate your second language acquisition. Being able to determine the meaning of words because you have an expansive vocabulary will save you time and energy in the short, medium, and long term. While fluency will require far more than pattern recognition and extensive knowledge, it cannot set you back. If you are looking for a place to start, there are some things you can start doing immediately to catapult yourself forward.

1. Look at prefixes and suffixes

2. Look at root words

3. Read often to expand your vocabulary

Above all, if you are going to do these things you need to write them down. Fluency is not simply the ability to speak, it is also the ability to write and read and understand what people are saying to you. When you write down phrases you learn and practice your listening comprehension actively, you are contributing to your fluency, even if it does not feel like it. Every new word, every advancement in your comprehensible input, every successful self-evaluation is a step in the right direction towards fluency. Learning a foreign language cannot be done without taking the time to develop several language skills, but that does not mean you should not enjoy yourself throughout the process.

As a demonstration, I want to provide a deeper insight into pattern recognition within language acquisition by showing you what we do in my private courses with the Spanish language. This is incomplete and there are hundreds of patterns not listed here, but it should at least give you an idea of where to start and how you can make patterns a part of your second language acquisition irrespective of which language you are learning. This is what it looks like:

Of all the verbs you can and should learn, the verb for "to go" is going to be vital to your long term success. The reason for this is simple, it will help you express yourself in a new tense without having to learn a new conjugation for each word.
      There is a tense in Spanish called the "near future" and it will allow you to express your future intentions without having to learn the future tense conjugations. Fortunately, or unfortunately, this will be your first glimpse of irregular verb conjugations. Let's take a look.

Jumping Ahead: Spanish Examples

Conjugating "to go"

To go = ir

Yo voy
Tu vas
El/Ella/Usted va
Nosotros vamos
Ellos/Ellas/Ustedes van

Great! But how does this translate into expressing a new tense? Let's work through some translations. When we express the "near future" in English, it looks like this:

I am going to eat at the restaurant.
You are going to travel.
He is going to drive the car.
We are going to walk together.
They are going to give us a present.

It works the same way in most languages, Spanish included. So let's see what they look like on top of one another. Remember, in most romance languages you do not need to add the pronoun. The conjugation and context will tell the people you are speaking to who the subject is. Finally, when using the "near future" you will need to add "a" before the infinitive of the verb you are "going to" be doing.

I am going to eat at the restaurant.
(Yo) Voy a comer al restaurante.
You are going to travel.
(Tu) Vas a viajar.
He is going to drive the car.
(El/Ella/Usted) Va a conducir el coche.
We are going to walk together.
(Nosotros) Vamos a caminar juntos.
They are going to give us a present.
(Ellos/Ellas/Ustedes) Van a darnos un regalo.

Let's look at the formula:
Ir (conjugated) a + infinitive verb + context

Write it down and practice it often. Do not be afraid to make mistakes, just practice.

Loan words are words that the English language takes from Spanish and uses as their own. Every language has these and as you get deeper into your language learning experience you will notice that there are English words Spanish speakers use as their own as well.
      This happens with nouns, verbs, adjectives, and adverbs alike, so whenever you come across them you need to be writing them down. In order to remember these things, you will have to use them. Additionally, if you are really struggling to come up with the word you need, using brands or adding "o", as is the cliché, works more often than one might think.

More on that later, though. For now, here are some examples:

- Llama	- Potato	- Tobacco
- Yucca	- Barbecue	- Hurricane
- Bronco	- Desperado	- Rodeo
- Vigilante	- Avocado	- Banana
- Burrito	- Maiz	- Chili
- Dorado	- Margarita	- Tequila
- Tortilla	- Yam	- Vanilla
- Guacamole	- Papaya	- Pimiento
- Adobe	- Savvy	- Siesta
- Fiesta	- Embargo	- Tornado
- Barracuda	- Alfalfa	- Algebra
- Cafeteria	- Canyon	- Macho
- Mosquito	- Jaguar	- Incommunicado
- Guitar	- Cigar	- Renegade
- Alligator	- Armadillo	- Alcove
- Albino	- Camping	- Fútbol
- Básquetbol	- Tenis	- Rugby
- Goal	- Comic	- Okay
- Patio	- Comrade	- Cargo
- Coyote	- Armada	- Pronto

Stereotypes come from somewhere. Paying attention to the things people assume is often a good way to get started. It will not *always* work, though. You will be more likely to remember the times it does not work when you get used to things going well. Mistakes will stand out and you will have a much better chance of remembering the things you are learning.

With that in mind, remember that you will encounter different ways to say the same things, so going forward, even if these stereotypes work out, try to find new and more eloquent ways to say the same things.

Let's take a look at all the words in Spanish where the "add an -o" to the end trope actually works:

- Carro	- Minuto	- Segundo
- Excepto	- Caso	- Archivo
- Plato	- Médico	- Calendario
- Secreto	- Acento	- Perfecto
- Descreto	- Elemento	- Directo
- Sincero	- Tímido	- Rápido
- Obeso	- Mucho	- Absoluto
- Entero	- Crítico	- Documento
- Momento	- Honesto	- Necesario
- Concreto	- Intenso	- Lógico
- Explosivo	- Contrario	- Primero
- Político	- Experto	- Típico
- Adjetivo	- Adverso	- Verbo
- Banco	- Diagnóstico	- Tecnológico
- Público	- Gráfico	- Solo

This particular trick works exceptionally well with words that have the -ism or -ive suffix in English. You will also find that many fields of study within the sciences share this ending often changing from —logist to —logo, an example being psychologist and psicólogo. As you get deeper into your language acquisition, you will see how often it works and, again, you will find out there are times when it simply does not. Mistakes are inevitable, but if you are learning from them then they are going to be beneficial rather than detrimental.

When a word in Spanish ends with -ado or -ido, it indicates past tense. However, when you are describing things, people, or places, it is the equivalent of adding -ed. Let's take a look:

Spanish: English:

- Terminado   - Terminated
- Invitado   - Invited
- Obligado   - Obliged
- Acelerado   - Accelerated
- Acumulado   - Accumulated
- Alternado   - Alternated
- Enamorado   - Enamored
- Apreciado   - Appreciated
- Adaptado   - Adapted
- Abandonado   - Abandoned
- Anticipado   - Anticipated
- Articulado   - Articulated
- Clasificado   - Classified
- Compensado   - Compensated
- Complicado   - Complicated

The reason that ado/ido adds an -ed to the word in English is because it is a form of the past tense in Spanish. While this guide is not meant to teach grammar in any way, there is no way around it when you go deep enough. Experiment with these words and as you learn new verbs, keep in mind the possibilities of these patterns in that endeavor. We only made it to the "E"s leaving the "F"s through the "Z's" to be discovered!
    You will not be correct every single time you use them, but it will work often enough that is worth trying out. If you cannot think of one way, try another. For example, you may choose to say "enamored" instead of "in love" because enamored follows the "drop -ed and add -ado to the end" rule. Many words have synonyms and if you can pinpoint which word corresponds closest with its Spanish counterpart, you will find learning Spanish is not all too difficult after all.
Another thing you are going to need when speaking Spanish is access to adverbs.

These words describe verbs and in English many of them end in -ly. Fortunately, this crosses over into Spanish with the suffix -mente. Here's what it looks like:

Spanish: English:

- Exactamente   - Exactly
- Solamente   - Solely
- Normalmente   - Normally
- Fortunatamente   - Fortunately
- Intensamente   - Intensely
- Absolutamente   - Absolutely
- Honestamente   - Honestly
- Necesariamente   - Necessarily
- Principalmente   - Principally
- Rápidamente   - Rapidly
- Simplemente   - Simply
- Totalmente   - Totally
- Diligentemente   - Diligently
- Completamente   - Completely

    These are just a few examples of how you can use your pattern recognition skills to expand and improve your vocabulary and grammar. However, you can also use patterns to ameliorate your accent if you know how to do it.

    Accents come from somewhere, often it has a lot to do with the alphabet in each respective language. For this, the focus will be on the ESL, or English as a Second Language, habit that many Spanish speakers have. Adding an "e" to the beginning of words that begin with "s" is common and demonstrates just how important it is to master the alphabet **and** expand your vocabulary, even in English. You may encounter a Spanish speaker pronouncing school as "eschool" and that is because the word in Spanish is escuela. Scribe is another word for writer in English, the word in Spanish for "write" is "escribir" The word for "study" in Spanish is "estudiar" For "student" it is "estudiante" you see?

Use this as often as you can, it won't always work, but when it does you will make great strides.

Aside from basic phrase patterns, there are patterns within the very alphabet that can make the biggest difference. Once you understand how different languages interact, having an accent is suddenly far less of an issue. Besides, an accent is nothing more than a sign of bravery. That said, of course the end goal is always to sound like a native speaker and with enough effort you can make that happen.

There are many ways to address an accent. The best way by far when you are starting out is to over exaggerate the things you are saying. This is especially true when working with the "R" in most languages. While there are several issues that different languages present when it comes to speaking fluidly, the "R" in most languages is complex to master. If you are struggling with this letter, or any letter for that matter, then you should be speaking it in an exaggerated manner. Once you master the sound and how it interacts in different contexts you can begin to refine and zero in on the native speaker accent we all seek to achieve.

In order to do this you will want to have something to mimic. Whether it is music, audiobooks, podcasts, movies, or something else, having a voice you enjoy that you can mimic is helpful. More importantly, though, having the voice recorded so you can go back and listen to it over and over again will be imperative. It is fantastic to converse with people, but the rate of speed at which conversation takes place is rarely conducive to accent training. The more input data you have to work with the better. In fact, the more emphasis you put on complex words and approaching problems from different angles the easier this will be.

While practicing basic phrases is great, correct output is just as important as massive input. When you are just getting started you are going to find that your input far outweighs your output. That is okay, but eventually you want to be producing. The more you speak, the more you write, the faster and more thorough your language acquisition will be.

Your brain works best when you develop your own pattern recognition systems and pronunciation is a part of that. As you practice pattern identification you will find that you unlock methods to ameliorate your accent all on your own.

However, there is one thing that works better than most other activities. That said, it requires you to step outside of the beginning stages of second language acquisition. Grammar is important, but you do not speak grammar. You speak vocabulary. Grammar drills tend to make people even more fearful of speaking depending on the context. If you can master complex words and read them fluidly you will, at the very least, not be afraid of making mistakes when you speak. Will you still make mistakes? Absolutely, yes. But you will also have a mountain of confidence simply from the ability to speak without hesitation. Fortunately seeking out difficult and complex words often means you will be enveloped in interesting content and this alone will enhance and accelerate your second language acquisition.

The quality of your input will inevitably lead to the quality of your output, for better or worse. If you intend to have the capacity to give a quality description, you need to add that vocabulary to your knowledge base. Often people feel that they are incapable of describing how they feel in an accurate and eloquent way, even this is enough to stop people from trying.

That is not the goal, you want a better representation of yourself than that. Learning to speak fluidly, until you can lose your accent entirely, will help you get to this point. However, accent corrective activities are rarely defined. If you have nothing to refer to then starting the process can be nearly impossible. Here are some things you can do today to develop your own accent pattern recognition systems.

One of the most enjoyable ways to practice your accent in your target language is through lyric music videos. Aside from finding new music to fall in love with, you will be able to see precisely how different words can be pronounced. Understanding that pronunciation is malleable will hopefully shape your view of speaking in a positive way. The ability to see multiple pronunciation techniques before choosing one is important because often students are too focused on pronouncing things in an identical manner to their teachers. This is rarely the best way forward. You do not share a brain with your educator and speaking identically to them will rarely serve you in a positive way. Aside from the restraint of only being able to learn what they know, you risk mispronouncing things because *they* mispronounce things.

Interesting content can be found anywhere. Believe it or not, some of the most unique vocabulary can be found in songs. In fact, if you pay close enough attention people will be more impressed by your vast vocabulary than disappointed in your accent. Once when I was in Belgium I was talking to someone about a song I loved and they did not think the lyrics made sense. That is because he did not know the words that were being used and once we looked them up together he could not believe how large my vocabulary was. It will be like this for you, too, irrespective of your accent. Besides, the only person who cares about your accent is you. Most people only care about communication and if you can communicate then nothing else really matters.

Music is great, but after a certain amount of time it can be difficult to study it. Eventually you will just want to listen and enjoy. Once you get to that point it is time to move to the next method. Of course, never underestimate the power of music, people learn new words in their native languages every day simply by listening to talented lyricists and musicians. If you need a break, though, reading aloud is the next best option. It does require a bit more attention, but if you put emphasis on interesting content you will have no problems.

Reading aloud is a fantastic method to improve your accent and overall speaking in your target language. Normally when you are speaking the most difficult part is coming up with words ahead of time. By the time you make your comment it is entirely possible that the conversation has moved on to a new subject. When you read aloud, though, this is not an issue. Rather than process what is being said, you can focus all of your energy on the pronunciation and tempo of your speech. Reading aloud is speaking with training wheels.

Once you get used to reading aloud and having solo conversations, your next move is to begin conversing with people as often as possible. Whether that be people with whom you work, friends in foreign countries, or random people on a gaming server, conversation is absolutely necessary. Aside from being good with regards to colloquial language, you will also learn how words sound when they are spoken by native speakers. Often the way things are written is nowhere near the way they are spoken. A simple example of this is the French for "I do not know". Here is what it looks like:

English: I don't know

French, written: Je ne sais pas

French, as taught in public education: Je ne sais pas

French, as spoken by native speakers: Jsais pas (pronounced "djay paw")

This is not the only example, there are many, but this illustrates the idea well. Most native speakers shorten the words they use and this can be devastating to a new language learner if they have never encountered it before.

Here are a few examples in English so you can visualize:

- **Gonna**

- **Shoulda/Coulda/Woulda**

- **Bro/Sis/Ma/Pa**

Some languages have more than others, French is particularly egregious, but that does not mean it is uncommon in other languages. Having conversations with people will make these patterns more recognizable and the ability to ask for clarification is extremely helpful. Unsupervised learning is difficult, but it is far from impossible. All it means is explanations will be harder to come by and getting an accurate measure of your proficiency may be difficult.

  However, if you give your brain lots to do and example after example approaching from different angles then you should not have any issues. You may be lacking complicated grammatical explanations, but you will also benefit from the ability to recognize familiar patterns quickly. The more emphasis you put on pattern classification the easier it will be for you to notice patterns and this is just as important in ameliorating your accent as it is in progressing in different languages. There is no reason to be ashamed of your accent. Seeking to speak like a native speaker is fantastic, it is a great goal, but at no point should having an accent hold you back from communicating with people. People want to speak with you, they will not care if you sound a little funny. In fact, in many cases having an accent will make people *more* likely to help you.

  Of course, if you want to fix your accent then you are going to have to actively work towards fluency. Practicing complex words, singing along to music videos, and reading aloud are all things that are conducive to the goal of speaking like a native. That said, you cannot avoid conversations if you are serious about this. People want to communicate with you and if you want to speak perfectly you will need to start speaking as soon as possible. Expecting perfection from the beginning is a fool's errand. Started is better than perfect every time. It is not possible to perfect something you have not started.

Conclusion

In bringing this all to a conclusion I want to discuss some things you can start doing today to begin your language acquisition anew. Best practices, first steps, and for those who have a second language or two under their belt already, some techniques for managing two or more languages. In conjunction with everything up until now, you will be able to build a language learning curriculum that is unique to you so that you can all but guarantee your long term success.

Different techniques work for different people and a one size fits all approach is never conducive to success. However, these best practices will work irrespective of your learning style, age, or prior knowledge. That is why they are best practices. The differentiation will come in how you apply the practice and which forms of comprehensible input you choose to work with during the different stages of your language acquisition. At the end of the day your goal is going to be getting as much exposure as physically possible, but if you always approach it the same way you will not be prepared for real life situations. Nothing is cookie cutter. Every interaction you have will be unique and if you fail to prepare you will struggle to work with native speakers when the time comes.

There are components of language acquisition you need to be hitting on every day in order to assure you are a well rounded language learner. While you can certainly focus on one over the others, it is important to train yourself in everything to eliminate any weak points in your language skills. It's never fun to say, "Well I can understand everything, but I can't really speak." There are 5 components to know.

They are, in short:

- **Reading**
- **Writing**
- **Speaking**
- **Listening**
- **Translating**

    Whether it's a public or private school, homeschool, or self taught, managing these 5 elements is vital for successful language acquisition. While there are plenty of ways to make these things happen, sometimes something so vast can be difficult to nail down. Homeschool families and solo language studies have a difficult enough task without trying to sort through all of the information the internet has to offer and public schools rarely take advantage of things that don't drive standardized tests.

    Unfortunately for the student that usually leads to students attempting to focus on test results rather than language acquisition. It also means that public and private schools tend to gear the student's education towards scoring higher on standardized tests rather than learning the language. That is not your goal. Your goal is to master a new language and be able to speak to anyone at any time about any subject. For that to happen here are the things you can, and should, focus on within each component.

Reading

When working on reading it is often tempting to only stick to things that can be understood 100%, but this is to the detriment of the student's education. One thing people seem to forget is that there are very few books that can be read without learning new words. Even as an adult, if someone is learning new words as an adult every time they read, there is no reason to think that it's necessary to understand everything being read in a foreign language. It will come, but it is vital to continue reading irrespective of whether or not you or your children understand every word.

While it will be painstaking, reading difficult literature is a phenomenal way to improve. That said, even comics often have plenty of words and phrases that are worth knowing. They also provide a window into the culture of the countries where the target language is spoken. The greatest advantage, though, is that there are infinite resources out there for just about any subject at virtually every level available for free online. As simple as it sounds, sometimes the best time to make this happen is by just reading about things you are interested in written in your target language. If you need help finding some materials, please do not hesitate to reach out! Resources are vital for homeschooled children and homeschooling parents, but even if you're not homeschooling, I am always happy to help hunt down some extra resources for you to use.

Writing

Something that can be done without any resources, on the other hand, is writing. I talk about writing all the time with the people I work with and it's for a simple reason, to enhance recall ability. At the end of the day, the ability to speak comes from the ability to recall words swiftly and accurately. Without speaking, there are very few ways to train this, however, writing is a perfect way to practice. The way memory works, the more senses that go into something the better it is encoded and the easier it is to recall later. So, if you hear a word, you might remember it. If you hear and see a word, you're slightly more likely to remember it. If you hear, see, and write a word, you're even more likely to remember it. Then if you hear, see, write, and say the word, you give yourself the best chance at being able to recall it later.

Writing even 5 sentences per day is good enough to get things moving in the right direction, but the more you write the better you will read. There is something else, though, that can help with both of these things.

Listening

When it comes to listening, there are ways to make auditory stimulus sessions more effective, but oftentimes just having ample passive listening will be good enough. What you'll notice is that as long as you are reading and constantly learning new words, even passive listening will yield results as you will understand more and more each time. Audiobooks are excellent for this and most public domain books are available for free on YouTube and other platforms.
When attempting to create an environment of localized immersion, ensuring that there are ample resources for you to go along at your own pace. Generally, I recommend attempting to replace one thing per week that you do in your native language with something you do in your target language.
For example, if you usually listen to sports highlights in your native language, start listening to them in your target language.
     If you usually listen to the news in your native language, listen to the news in your native language, start listening to music in your target language.
This change is simple, but small, consistent, changes move entire mountains. The same goes for everything, not just listening and auditory stimuli. Slowly replacing your native language with your target language is the goal of localized immersion. That is the best way to integrate language learning into your homeschool journey.

Speaking

As far as stimulus goes, speaking is the most difficult for the most people. However, if there is no option then it becomes slightly easier to facilitate. When fully immersed, there is no way out. That is what the goal is for this idea of localized immersion. During the hour or two hours or however long per day that you are doing language work, there should be absolutely zero interaction with your native language. This goes double for anyone you are teaching as it is vital to the child's education. Public schools fail at this and it is one of the reason so few people have been able to pick up a second language in public or private schools.

If the stressor is that words and pronunciation don't make complete sense, I encourage you to work with audiobooks and just repeat after the orator. Mimicking voices is a phenomenal way to hone an accent and work towards being mistaken for a native speaker.

Translating

Translation is a hugely underrated tool in learning a second language. The more you translate things, the better you understand how your target language relates to and interacts with your native language. If you can understand the patterns then learning will be smooth and quick. That said, it is a significantly tolling endeavor. There is a reason that many people make a good living as translators or interpreters.

Focusing on translating even a single page per day will make the next study session even more effective. I did this and I understand how painstaking it can be and how tedious it can feel. That's what it's like drilling down the basics. But without the basics as a sound foundation it is impossible to build anything worthwhile. I still use a physical dictionary when I am doing translations simply because looking up the words makes it more likely that I will remember the words.

With these in mind, implementation can *feel* more complex or at the very least more overwhelming. In an effort to overcome this, sometimes the best solution is the k.i.s.s or keep it simple stupid methodology. You can easily convince yourself that everything in front of you is insurmountable, but that does not have to be the case. With that said, having loose (or strict) rules to follow during the education process can provide the perfect guardrails to lead to success. With that in mind, I thought about all of the things that I try to keep in mind when creating lessons, building frameworks, and progressing my own language acquisition. These are the 10 commandments of second language acquisition according to the Second Language Strategies methodology.

1. Add new vocabulary words every single day

The age-old debate between vocabulary and grammar will likely never end. Primarily because different things work for different people and, at the end of the day, you need both. That said, without a vocabulary you will never have the chance to practice your grammar, so inundating yourself with new vocabulary on a daily basis is a must.

It could be 5 words, it could be 10 words, it could be 50 words like my students do. Irrespective of what you choose, so long as you are consistent you will see results over time. Write them down, say them aloud, work them into sentences, do everything you can to ensure they are solidified in your memory. That includes returning to them to review weekly so you are not spending time learning things just to forget them.

2. Always ask questions

Reading is one of the best things you can do to bolster your second language acquisition and the reason why may shock you. It is not for the vocabulary or the grammar or the information you are reading about, it's because it will, theoretically, cause you to start asking questions. Pay attention to how things are worded, ask yourself these questions:

How does it compare to your native language?

Can you move the words around in your native language to emulate the target language?

Does it sound awkward if you do?

Are there other ways to express this exact sentiment?

Are there words that resemble words in your native language? What do they mean?

How can you add these things into your lexicon? Is there something you would add or remove to make it sound better?

Where does this word come from? What about this sentence structure?

These are just a few examples you can use to bolster your reading time. At the end of the day, the more you train yourself to question things the easier it will be to maximize your curiosity.

3. Immerse yourself

One of the core tenants of language acquisition is immersion. It could be complete, partial, or simulated, but it needs to be there. When you are learning a new language you need to be exposed to it. The more time you spend exposed to the language the quicker you will reach a point where you are able to speak and hold conversations..

4. Take every opportunity you get

This is probably the most intimidating aspect of language acquisition, but it is something you must do if you want to be successful. Depending on where you live and what language you are learning you are going to have a variety of opportunities to speak your new language. In order to be successful you need to take as many of these opportunities as possible.

Theory is great, but it is meaningless without practice. It can be extremely difficult to know what you do not know if you neglect practice. When you speak, there is no hiding behind theory. You can either do it or you cannot. If you cannot, you now know what you need to work on and you can devise a plan of attack to destroy any inadequacies.

5. Make mistakes

Hand in hand with taking every opportunity is making mistakes. It may not be the most enjoyable, but learning from your mistakes is certainly the most effective. Most people may think it is great to go the whole time without making any mistakes, but in all likelihood those people are not making mistakes because they are not pushing themselves. There is a huge difference between do what you are good at and do it flawlessly.

Millions of people around the world make mistakes in their native language every single day. Some people make so many mistakes that entirely new words are created and added to dictionaries. Do not fear mistakes, they are part of the game. The more you make now the fewer you will make a year from now when you are speaking your new language with native speakers. However, in order to get to that point you need to have goals.

6. Set goals

Goal setting is paramount for success in almost every aspect of life. Without a target to aim at it can be almost impossible to remember where you are headed. Fortunately, your goals are no longer determined by outside forces like the public education system. You can set your own goals, your own milestones, and your own deadlines. That said, with so much freedom often comes a bit of paralysis through analysis. Make sure your goals are attainable, on a timeline, measurable, and relevant to you.

7. Track your progress

Having goals is great, but you also need to be tracking your progress. Truth is, if you spent years in the gym, but neglected to track the numbers, you left progress on the table. The same goes for learning anything. While I am not a fan of the way public schools go about this, it is an absolutely crucial element in ensuring consistent progress.

8. Be well rounded

One of the most common phrases used by people who tried and gave up on language acquisition is, "I can read and understand the language, but I cannot speak it." and that, to me, is tragic. It is certainly normal, but if you make the decision to not walk away, you will never experience this particular problem. Being a well rounded learner means attacking each component of second language acquisition.
　　　You cannot just listen to music and watch TV, you need to read, you need to speak, you need to write, you need to translate. When you hit all of these consistently you will slowly begin to **think** in your target language which will make it exponentially easier to **speak** your target language. If you are constantly thinking in English, your sentence structure and vocabulary will suffer for it.

9. Speak early and often

It is possible that the biggest failure of the public education methodology falls here. Students are rarely, if ever, encouraged to actually speak the language. It does not have to be in the first week, it does not have to be in the second week, but by the third week you should be at the very least speaking two or three sentences every time you sit down to work on your language.

There are plenty of ways to go about this, from reading aloud to writing your own sentences and speaking them. It does not matter where you start, only that you start. Once you can put one sentence together try putting two sentences together. Then try to go for three and four consecutive sentences. Answer questions, ask questions, talk about the things you know and enjoy.

Get used to uncomfortable silence and do **not** give yourself a way out. It is easy to say, "well, I don't know, I guess I'll Google the answer" but easy is not effective. If you do not know the precise way to say something, find another way. Use what you do know to express what you don't know and then build on it. You can use your basic understanding to improve your precision and eloquence over time.

Again, though, if you are not doing this and making mistakes you will continue to struggle as you fail to understand the issues you have. You may want to feel perfect, but perfection means there is no room for growth. I promise you, even in your native language you have several opportunities for improvement. Have you ever let that stop you from speaking your native language?

10. Go beyond your level

The final commandment from SLS is to always push to go beyond your purported language learning level. I may have said the 9th commandment is where public schools miss the most, but in reality it is more likely this. There is absolutely no reason you should be spending years on end learning to use three verb tenses. You should be able to discuss your hobbies and different current events by the end of year two, not just numbers, colors, and animals.

Irrespective of what you think your language level is, you should be using input that is decidedly above that level. If you are an A1 student, you should be working with B1 input. Staying in A1 material tends to result in staying at the A1 level. If you want to improve you need to be doing progressively more difficult tasks.

You are in control of your education now, but that freedom can be suffocating if you don't know what you are doing. These are our 10 commandments, but if one of them does not work for you, then don't use it. If you do all of these things, you will become bilingual, but there is more than one path to the destination. Do what works for you, but do not let that act as an excuse to avoid pushing yourself in the realms of speaking, writing, and translating. That said, fighting to get above your level is easier said than done. So here are some ways you can level up right now and implement the final commandment in your day to day language learning routine.

Going above your level

Someone the other day told me that there is no way to discuss philosophy after only learning a new language for a few months. While it certainly is not normal, to say it is impossible is just plain wrong. When it comes to second language acquisition, outside of mainstream classrooms the limitations that are placed on you will be placed on you by yourself, not by anyone else. So long as you do not impose limits because of something someone else says, the opportunities are endless. That said, taking the leap from Duolingo and children's books to classic literature and documentaries may *feel* like a larger jump than it actually is if you try to do it without a plan.

Once you have mastered the alphabet and put some work into laying a strong foundation of new vocabulary words, it is time to step it up. You do not have to do all of these things, but adding even a few into your weekly rotation will enhance and accelerate your second language acquisition. Adding additional layers to each piece of comprehensible input will increase the likelihood that everything available to you in your short term memory is also being committed to your long term memory. It is certainly more labor intensive, but it will also take less time overall to accomplish your language learning goals.

The first thing you can do is start reading high level books. By that I mean exploring the classics from every corner of the world. Starting out, try and read a book you know well in your native language.

When you do not have to spend all of your time trying to follow the story or get to know the characters you can spend more time focused on the language itself. Much of the most recent discussions have been about increasing your language output, but for this we will really zero in on comprehensible input.

Reading comprehension is important, but being able to turn your time reading into dedicated study time is probably more important. Knowing how and when to pick out and commit new vocabulary words to your memory, understanding how to make sense of different grammar structures, and creating a system to categorize verbs and their conjugations will enhance and accelerate your second language acquisition. For that reason the higher level the book the more benefit you will likely get from it.

Working through these books with a dedicated language learning notebook is vital. You need a written record of all the things you are learning if you want to commit things to memory. Whenever you run into moments of deflation where you feel like you are lacking motivation, having these notes and vocabulary words and grammar explanations written down will give you a way to breathe new life into your second language acquisition. Momentum is powerful, but it is easier to take advantage of momentum that has at least some physical form, even if it's only written language. Outside of reading, watching documentaries is a great way to challenge your purported language level. You can start doing this as early in your journey as you want, but ideally you will have at least a solid base of vocabulary words at your disposal. This will give you a little breathing room when things start to move a bit too quickly.

In most documentaries, especially those filmed in your target language, the narrators are going to be native speakers. However, unlike real life situations, the narrators of documentaries make concerted efforts to speak well and annunciate intentionally. While it can be dangerous to become reliant on this sort of stimulus, it is a great way to develop your listening skills without struggling with the normal tempo and dialect of a native speaker. Once you get outside of this type of learning environment you will have to work hard again to understand multiple people speaking at various tempos and pitches. To mitigate this, do what you can to diversify the input you work with from day to day.

On the days when you are feeling less confident, return to the narrators who are easiest for you to understand and start building your confidence back up. Whenever you are having a tough time feeling confident, go back and do the things you **know** you are good at for a time. As you work to get beyond the need for subtitles, this will be more important than ever. Listening to a foreign language without subtitles is absolutely exhausting and can be soul crushing. The only thing you really have to do to make it easier on yourself is listen to whatever your input of choice is twice. One time through and you may get some words, but the second time through will often prove easier to understand. Each time through will provide you with new words and you will quickly reach a point where you understand the first time through.

Escaping subtitles is your final challenge with audiovisual input. Once you can understand the things being said without reading them you will be able to go out confidently ready to speak to anyone and everyone. Avoid always listening to the same person whether it be audiobooks, documentaries, or telenovelas, diversifying the content you consume is crucial. Many people often struggle because they learned to understand the way their instructor spoke only to find out that there are thousands of cadences, tones, and voices that do **not** sound the same.

When it comes to second language acquisition, there's a reason that having an immersion environment complete with native speakers is the best method. What few people ever discuss, however, is that the immersion method is also the most difficult irrespective of which of the many foreign languages you are learning. At the end of a full immersion day you will be exhausted. You will feel lost and useless and hopeless often, but it is all worth it. Doing difficult things will make your future easier. Whether that is going to the gym to move heavy objects or choosing to work at the end of the day rather than watch TV and scroll through social media at night, doing difficult things makes the future easier. Choosing to turn away from comfort and embrace struggle will enhance and accelerate your second language acquisition. The best thing you can do is consistently find ways to challenge yourself.

Dictation is the best way to challenge yourself with any piece of comprehensible input. You will need the audio and a transcript or subtitles, but you will not read the transcript or subtitles. Listen to whatever it is, ideally form some native speakers, and write down the things you *think* you are hearing. Often you will find that what you think you hear and what you do hear are two different things. Running this test on yourself consistently will lay bare your foreign language skills. This, again, is where taking the time to listen two or even three times will be beneficial.
In all likelihood you *will* miss some words the first time through. Whether the sentence or paragraph is context dependent will determine whether or not you need to go back

through, but there is no shame in running it back when necessary. You won't be able to replay someone's words when speaking to them in a real life situation, so take the advantage you have when studying alone to do it.

Depending on your definition, it is absolutely possible to learn a new language quickly. It will take months, but it does not have to take years. If you only do Duolingo and listen to some music from time to time then yes, it will take longer than it should.

As you push yourself to do more and more challenging things, the things many people would try to convince you are "above" your "level", you will find that you are able to accomplish more than you initially believed. Every challenge you overcome will bolster your confidence and make it easier for you to start speaking when the time comes. Any mistakes you make while studying are mistakes you are far less likely to make when using the language in your day to day life. That is also the risk of *not* challenging yourself. You will play how you practice, so do not shy away from high intensity practice. It will be exhausting, but once you have it down you will be able to build in ways to be more efficient in all that you do. You are capable of doing more than you think and until you try you will never know. Don't forget, though, the best you can do now is not the best you will ever be able to do.

When you get to the point where you have a second language under your belt you might need to find ways to manage multiple languages. Once you have the itch for language learning it can be difficult to do away with, but that is a good problem to have. There are nearly countless languages available for you to conquer, but each will bring a new challenge. Fortunately there are tried and true methods that can help you with each subsequent language. Much of it is the same, but it will definitely require a unique approach for each individual.

Managing and Learning Multiple Languages

There are many people who prefer to work on multiple foreign languages simultaneously. While there are pros and cons to consider when taking this approach to developing your language skills, if you plan to speak more than two languages it is going to be vital that you develop strategies to juggle the new languages. From keeping the new vocabulary words separate to ensuring your grammar structures are staying consistent, learning more than one language at a time is going to be challenging. If you do it right, though, you might find that each new language is just a tool to learn something new.

The first thing people usually struggle with when approaching multiple languages at the same time is determining how much time to dedicate to each language. At the end of the day, an even split tends to be best for most people. While it can feel as though you would be better off spending more time with the language you knew least, this can quickly become counterproductive. Frustration is a feeling all language learners have experienced at least once in their journey. Working on the language you know best at least as often as you work on your third language can do wonders when you feel like you want to give up. It does not have to be the same type of studying, either. Much of what you will do at the later stages of learning a new language is different from the things you will do at the beginning or intermediate stages. The comprehensible input will look vastly different for both languages assuming you do not have a similar level in both.

Here are some ways to get **high level** comprehensible input in your day to day life to ensure you are consistently advancing in your better second language:

1. Put Your Listening to the Test

If you are at the point where you are working on two languages at the same time, chances are you know one of them better than the other. For that language, listening and reading are going to be highly important. This is primarily due to the fact that you can spend less time actively working on this particular language so you need to prioritize things that you can do passively while also assuring you will consistently be challenged. Podcasts and audiobooks are your best bet for this. Anyone who is working on Spanish, French, or German can check out these audiobook playlists we put together over on YouTube. If you are working on something else, keep in mind that many of the classics are available for free as audiobooks on YouTube.

Getting constant exposure should be your top priority for the better language. Building a learning environment centered around immersion is key and will give you a little breathing room when you are feeling overwhelmed by everything else life has to offer.

2. Cultivate relationships with native speakers

At this point, it is time to start seeking outside help from native speakers. The silent period of second language acquisition is painful enough without experiencing it in several languages at once. If you are still struggling to speak this is the time to step outside of your comfort zone. With how many concepts you will have to master, learning a new culture and new vocabulary words in context from a native speaker can make all the difference. Solo study is great and can be effective, but if you really want to learn a new language you probably want to be able to speak to native speakers. There is a certain contingent of people who will tell you that no matter what you do you will never keep up with native speakers, but do not let the limits they have placed on themselves stand in your way. Speaking with native speakers will bring you to a point where you can easily keep up with them. It is one of the only ways to learn new words that mainstream classrooms likely do not know exist.

3. Translations to master second language acquisition

This final step is not for the faint hearted. Of all the previous challenges you have likely faced, this will be the greatest. Translate the things you come across in your tertiary language into your secondary language. Ideally you will have already gotten into the habit of translating the things you come across in daily life from your native language to your new language, but if not you should be doing that as well. One of the reasons this works so well is that you are likely already doing it. When you start actively working to translate all of your comprehensible input you will more than likely struggle, at first. Over time, however, it will get easier. Keep in mind that the first time you do something it is going to take twice as long as each subsequent time. Do not let an hour long activity scare you away as it will likely take half that time after doing it for more than a week.
     Here are some ways to get **low level** comprehensible input in your day to day life to ensure you are consistently advancing in your better second language:

4. Using music to break the language barrier

Music is a universal language. Being able to talk about music is a phenomenal way to make new friends and explore a new culture. Not only that, but you will be put into contact with a myriad of new vocabulary words you can add to your repertoire. With how often lyrics turn into common spoken language it is often well worth your time to invest into watching some lyric videos at least 3 times throughout the week. Irrespective of which language you are learning, exposure is key. The level of exposure is what you will want to change and deciding what you want to take on as far as comprehensible input goes is where the differentiation will occur. You might find audiobooks too challenging in your weakest language, but music is perfect. Once you are feeling everything is too easy to understand then it is time to level up. As per usual, the 80% comprehension threshold is a good indication.

5. Reading out loud to master pronunciation

Theoretically, the language you consider "third" is the one you know the least. With that in mind, pronunciation and fluidity are great goals starting out. Seeking out beginner level books in your target language is a worthwhile endeavor and reading them aloud will improve your accent and fluidity while speaking. Your goal is simple when doing this, make it as long as possible without stuttering or needing to stop and repeat. This is easier said than done, but taking the time to do it is well worth it. Read through slowly first. Make sure each sentence flows together properly before moving on to the next. Once you get one perfect, add a second. From there add a third, then a fourth, and so on. Before you know it you will be able to read entire pages without thinking.

This, in essence, is speaking with training wheels because the words are already laid out for you. Eventually you will need to learn to **think** in your target language, but when you are just getting started and for the first few months, learning to speak fluidly and pronounce things well is vital. Laying a strong foundation upon which to build will ensure the latter half of your second language acquisition goes smoothly.

6. Take advantage of subtitles to enhance your language skills

Subtitles are probably the greatest invention for language learners worldwide in the past twenty years. Apps are great and all, but the ability to watch just about any piece of media with subtitles available in multiple languages is incredible. While the written language will not always be perfect and the translations often leave much to be desired, they are a great point of entry. Start with shows you know well and have already seen. Hearing the words in your new language while seeing how they correspond to vocabulary words in your first language will help with the subconscious process of learning a foreign language.

    By taking it back to shows you have already seen and know well you can spend less time trying to figure out the story and more time paying attention to which words are being used. Ideally this will also help you piece together how different languages look when they go from one to another. Since most of these do not involve writing, adding an extra layer to your work will be greatly beneficial. Writing is the first step in learning to **think** in your new language. Not only that, but it will help you commit the things you are learning to your working memory.

    You can, of course, do any of these things with your second, third, or fourth language and beyond. These splits are designed to help you ensure you are making the most of your time. As we age efficiency becomes far more important within the realm of second language acquisition. That is why juggling multiple languages effectively is so important. These activities are closely related, but some will work better than others for you, so try to maximize what works best for you. Anything that does not involve writing, though, will not be as effective as the other strategies listed above.

    Focusing on one language at a time is probably the best thing you can do. However, I know how tempting it can be to jump around, especially as your language skills improve. If you really want to focus on two languages at once and you are a native English speaker, it would likely benefit you to work on your English language skills. The better you know each language the better you can learn each subsequent language. This is especially true for written language as knowing the rules of your first language will help you as you learn the rules of a foreign language. Aside from that, all focus should be on building an immersion environment for yourself that is fluid in all the languages you are trying to learn. But learning and maintaining are different. Here are some ways you can manage and maintain the languages you do know while learning new ones simultaneously.

    Mixing up words and forgetting words is something that just about everyone who learns a second language experiences. The worst part is, most of the time, it doesn't happen until in the moment speaking with someone. All of a sudden the word is just gone, not only in the target language but also in the native language and any other language that's known. All this to say, if it happens to you it is completely normal and no, you are not losing your language. If working within a specific language family it is possible, and likely, that you will experience this at a higher rate. When I was learning French I would constantly confuse the Spanish and French words and it got even worse when I began to study Portuguese. These are things that are not unique to Romance languages, but that is where I felt it.

    What happened next I would not have believed had it not happen to me. I began to forget words in my native language. Suddenly I couldn't speak the language I had spoken for 18 years of my life and the other two I could speak I was barely able to hold conversations in at the time. I thought this was going to be something that I always dealt with and, to a certain extent, I was right. There are still times when I lose words and there are still times when I replace words in one language with words from another. However, after many years I have developed some strategies for keeping the languages separate.

- Read More

One of the best ways to begin compartmentalizing languages is by reading more. The more often you see and hear and use the word the less likely you are to use it in place of another word in another language, though this may not be true for your native language. Just five to ten pages every day in whichever languages you're working on will help. This is a strategy I use and one of the things I do that I think really helps is I read these pages back to back. Whether starting out reading comics and easier books or reading philosophy and the classics in the target languages, this will help in more ways than just compartmentalize languages.

- Switch as often as possible

This idea may seem slightly counterintuitive, but I have had great success using it. When I first started learning French, one of the greatest things that happened to me is I lived with a family where I spoke English with the mom and French with the dad. After just a few months I was able to switch back and forth seamlessly which only began to get difficult as I did it less and less.

With this in mind, switch back and forth on your language study days. Watch an episode in Spanish then watch it in French or German or Russian or whatever languages you're learning. Read ten pages in one language then read ten pages in the next language. Write 5 sentences in one language then write 5 sentences in the other language. Whatever you are doing, try to be doing it in whatever languages you're learning as quickly in succession as possible.

Fair warning, this is going to be difficult and extremely exhausting. However, if you stick with it then it will pay off in the long run. Even now I struggle when switching back and forth, but things always get smoother when I get back to practicing simultaneously. I wish I could say there was a simple cure or that I had the answer for how to make sure you'd never confuse words again, but I just can't say that. I do know, from my experience, that the more you switch the easier it gets to switch. Practice doesn't make perfect. Practice makes permanent.

Most of what I have to say about language acquisition has already been said, but I would like to end this book with some, hopefully, helpful words. As you are going through your journey there will be peaks and there will be valleys. It is vital for you to remember that the best you can be now is not the best you ever will be. I have walked hundreds of people through those valleys and most of the time the thing that gets them through it is understanding that they are not alone. At the end of the day, every single person who decides to learn a new language will feel inadequate, afraid, demoralized, and ready to give up. If that is something you are experiencing, it is crucial that you realize you are far from alone.

There is an entire education literature dedicated to the "silent period" of language acquisition which is essentially the time before you feel confident enough to speak. No one likes to make mistakes, but those who are willing to make mistakes make it much further than those who will only do things when they are perfect. Perfection is dangerous because it can cause paralysis through analysis which creates a negative feedback loop that can be difficult to break through. Do your best to prepare to make mistakes. Put it into context if you must. Every day millions upon millions upon millions of people butcher their native language and that has never once stopped those people from speaking. Do not allow a fear of mistakes prevent you from speaking because you will be making mistakes for years.

Making mistakes is part of life and you will learn more from your mistakes than from studying. The more you make and the sooner you make them the less time you will spend being afraid of miscommunication and butchering your new language. Public schools are essentially designed to destroy confidence, especially second language courses. If that is something you experienced, now is the time to take your power back. For better or worse, you are in control of your education from this moment on and you owe it to yourself to give yourself every possible advantage and set yourself up for success. In this book I have given you some ideas and tools you can use to enhance and accelerate your language acquisition. However, I cannot learn a language for you, no one but you can. It will be difficult, but you can do difficult things and be great, so go out and do difficult things and become great. I will be rooting for you.

At the back of this book you will find some additional pages that will hopefully be beneficial for you as you continue your language acquisition. Use them to take notes, track your resources, and ensure constant progression over time. If you have a family, consider that you can keep this as your dedicated language learning book to be shared with your loved ones whenever they embark on their own language learning journey.

Notes and Objectives

What:	By when:

List of Preferred Resources:

Throughout this journey, you will undoubtedly come across multiple resources that you really enjoy and plan to return to often.

However, these can be difficult to keep track of, especially over the course of months and years. Use this page to keep track of anything and everything you want to be able to come back to during your language acquisition.

Written	Audio	Video

WHAT I'M READING 📖

Reading Score Card	Unknown Words	Translations
Pages Today:		
Pages This Week:		
Pages Read Total:		
Books Read:		
Misc. Pages Read:		

Goal: Set and track reading goals. Use the provided chart to write down unknown words and their corresponding translations. Practice these words in this week's sentences!

WHAT I'M READING

Reading Score Card	Unknown Words	Translations
Pages Today:		
Pages This Week:		
Pages Read Total:		
Books Read:		
Misc. Pages Read:		

When researching these words, pay attention to the words being used to describe them. Even better, look up the definition in Spanish and see if you understand it!

WHAT I'M READING 📖

Unknown Words	Translations

Reading Score Card

Pages Today:

Pages This Week:

Pages Read Total:

Books Read:

Misc. Pages Read:

When researching these words, pay attention to the words being used to describe them. Even better, look up the definition in Spanish and see if you understand it!

WHAT I'M READING 📖

Reading Score Card	Unknown Words	Translations
Pages Today:		
Pages This Week:		
Pages Read Total:		
Books Read:		
Misc. Pages Read:		

When researching these words, pay attention to the words being used to describe them. Even better, look up the definition in Spanish and see if you understand it!

SENTENCES

10 (or more) words. Be sure to speak these out loud!!!

CORRECTIONS ✓

Use these pages to rewrite the previous week's sentences. How can you say these things better?

NOTES

NOTES:

NOTES

NOTES

Made in the USA
Columbia, SC
07 July 2024